LIBRARIES:
DREAMS, MADNESS, & REALITY

WALT CRAWFORD & MICHAEL GORMAN

American Library Association
Chicago and London
1995

Cover design by Tessing Design

The paper used in this publication meets the minimum
requirements of American National Standard for Information
Sciences—Permanence of Paper for Printed Library Materials,
ANSI Z39. 48-1992. ∞

Printed on 50-pound Glatfelter, a pH-neutral stock, and bound
in 10-point C1S cover stock by Malloy Lithographing, Inc.

Eureka and Zephyr are trademarks, and Ariel, CitaDel, and
RLIN are registered trademarks for products and services of The
Research Libraries Group, Inc. Other products and services
named in this book should be presumed to be trademarks of
their respective companies.

Quotation on p. 13 from "An Old Friend in a New Age," by Bob
Greene, *Chicago Tribune*, May 16, 1994. Used with permission.

Library of Congress Cataloging-in-Publication Data

Crawford, Walt.
    Future libraries : dreams, madness, and reality / Walt
Crawford and Michael Gorman.
      p.   cm.
    Includes bibliographical references and index.
    ISBN 0-8389-0647-8 (alk. paper)
    1. Libraries—United States—Automation.   2. Libraries
and electronic publishing—United States.   I. Gorman,
Michael, 1941– . II. Title.
Z678.A4U624   1995
025'.00285—dc20   94-43760

Printed in the United States of America.

99 98 97   5 4

Contents

Preface

Walt Crawford

My participation in this book began in 1992 when I was invited to speak at the Arizona State Library Association conference and those inviting me didn't have a specific topic in mind. The speech that emerged covered too much ground, but did point out some of the problems with an all-digital future and simplistic visions. My particular thanks to Mary Stout, the Library Automation Round Table, and ASLA for issuing the invitation and to all those who attended the October 1992 program "The Death of Print, Xanadu, and Other Nightmares, or, Brother, Can You Paradigm?"

Over years of reading, listening, and thinking, I had been aware that some silly and simplistic visions about the future of print and libraries emerged from time to time. More recently, such visions seemed to come from supposed leaders in the field and to be accepted by some librarians as "inevitable," without the librarians thinking through the bases for the visions and the consequences of the dreams. Their catchphrases—virtual library, universal workstation, buying back our own research, death of print—began to seem menacing as well as annoying, particularly when I began to hear of libraries with needed expansions threatened by people saying "but five years from now, there won't be any books to put on those new shelves."

I gave a few more speeches on various aspects of these problems, and noted some striking essays and articles in the area by Michael Gorman. We exchanged some notes (via Internet e-mail) and concluded that a joint project might make sense. This book is the result. Yes, of course we used the Internet and contemporary technology to do the book: just as there are no straw men in this book, there is no disdain for technology in its authors. We only met face-to-face twice (at Midwinter and Annual 1994); the contract negotiations, miscellaneous questions, and other issues were dealt with by e-mail, while writing and editing involved the U.S. Postal Service and Airborne Express (with diskettes and pages going between Fresno and Mountain View). Michael Gorman worked in WordPerfect 5.1 for DOS; I worked in Word for Windows 6.0, translating to Word for Windows 2.0 in order to prepare the Corel Ventura 4.2 pages. The joint authorship has been interesting and pleasurable.

In addition to the Arizona State Library Association, thanks should go to the Music Library Association, the University of Houston Libraries, the CLSI Eastern Region Users Group, Emory University Libraries and the University Circle, the Nevada Networking and Automation Group of the Nevada Library Association, AMIGOS, the Florida Library Association, and—especially—the Tennessee Library Association for inviting me to expand on some of the topics in this book.

My wife, Linda A. Driver, provided vital feedback throughout the process, bringing her perspective as a college library director to bear on the problems I was addressing. She also provided careful and thoughtful editing for the combined manuscript.

Early on, and more recently, several colleagues helped me to keep going with this project through extensive conversations that helped focus the issues in my mind: R. Bruce Miller, Sherrie Schmidt, Tom Wilson, Charles W. Bailey, Jr., Tamara Miller and Carol Parkhurst all come to mind, but I'm probably leaving out others who were equally helpful.

Finally, my thanks to Art Plotnik at ALA Editions for approving and guiding this project; to Dianne Rooney at ALA Publishing Services for helping me to develop and refine the book's design; and, of course, to Michael Gorman, for making this joint effort work so effortlessly (at least on my part).

Michael Gorman

My contribution to this book is formed by the many years in which I have worked in libraries and the large number of colleagues, some now dead, from whom I have learned about the realities of libraries and of the life of libraries. There seems never to have been a time in which libraries were not under one gun or another. There seems never to have been a time in which the actions of individual librarians were not inspired by dedication in the face of financial adversity and by the love of libraries. In all those years, the library has stood like a rock in the swift current of history—unchanging in its mission but always ready to try new ways of achieving that mission. Libraries are good things and the people who work in them do good work. If, in some small way, this book and my part in it can proclaim those truths and hearten those who believe in libraries and their future, then it will have been well worth the writing.

I would like to thank Walt Crawford for a most pleasant and productive collaboration and Art Plotnik for being a publisher with a heart and a keen editing eye. I would like to remember the late Frank Atkinson and the late Hugh Atkinson, two very different men who, at different times of my life, showed me how much libraries matter. I would like to acknowledge Eric Stone and Alan Thomas—teachers in the library school I attended 30 years ago—each of whom changed my professional life. It would be invidious to name just some of the many colleagues who have encouraged and inspired or just made me think—I hope they know who they are and how grateful I am. Last, I should mention the greatest blessing life has brought me, my daughters Emma Celeste Gorman and Alice Clara Gorman.

1

Credo

This book is about the present and the future of libraries.
We deal with the enduring values of libraries and librarianship and offer a vision of ways in which librarians may
use new ideas and new technologies to advance continuing
goals rooted in those values.

We believe in libraries. We believe in the enduring mission
of libraries. We believe that libraries and librarianship have a
future and that future is there to be seized by those with insight,
realism, and, yes, daring. This set of beliefs is rooted in practi-
cality and progressivism. Clinging to the past for the sake of the
past is as futile as sweeping away the past for the sake of a
delusionary future. We advocate a straight and narrow path
between the librarianship of nostalgia and the ill-informed
embrace of any technology that happens to capture the magpie
fancy of the moment.

This book looks back only to discern what is of permanent
value. It does so without nostalgia but with a true regard for the
accomplishments of those who have gone before. We look at
the present state of libraries—their triumphs and tribulations—
and cast a cold eye on the extrapolations of the present into the
unknown, if confidently predicted, future. We propose some
predictions of our own and hope that their bases in realistic
appraisals make them more credible than those of some techno-

futurists. Among other things, we want to add to the continuing dialog on the future of libraries and human communication.

Human Communication

Since the earliest years known to history, humankind has created records of its glories and follies in texts and images. Drawings on the walls of caves, signs made on the Azilian pebbles, the *quipus* (knotted strings) of Peru, the pictographs of the Dakota and other native Americans, marks made by incising stone or using a stylus to press wet clay, hieroglyphs, phonograms, ideographs, alphabets—all these are manifestations of the urge to communicate, record, and transfer knowledge, an urge that seems central to human identity.

With the art of writing, Carlyle said, an age of miracles began.[1] The ability to record thoughts and facts on portable objects (wood, clay, stone, metal, cloth, etc.) meant that human thought could defy space and time. Someone remote in place and removed by years could read the ideas of another person or the facts that person knew. There have been a number of innovations in the means by which knowledge and facts can be communicated—from papyrus rolls through print-on-paper, television, recorded sound, etc., to electronic texts. Each has enlarged on the original, fundamental breakthrough without changing its nature. Each has contributed to the annihilation of space by enabling people in remote locations to read writings in a shorter and shorter time after they are created.

On the other hand, because many innovations provide less durable records than their predecessors, time has regained its mastery.[2] What would we know of the library of Assurbanipal

---

1.   Thomas Carlyle, *The hero as divinity*, Lecture I of his *Heroes, hero-worship & the heroic in history*, Berkeley: University of California Press, 1993, p. 24. "It is the greatest invention man has ever made, this of marking down the unseen thought that is in him by means of written characters. It is a kind of second speech, almost as miraculous as the first."

2.   Hans Wellisch, "Aere perennius?" In *Crossroads: proceedings of the first national conference of the Library and Information Technology Association*, Chicago: American Library Association, 1984, pp. 22–34.

if, in the 7th century B.C., he had amassed electronic records rather than clay tablets?

Beyond space and time, the written communications of humankind have embodied the spirit of the human race and of the individual. As the book has evolved, so has the idea that "a good book is the precious life blood of a master spirit."[3] It has been said of a library and the writers whose work the library holds, "immortales animae in locis iisdem loquuntur" (*their immortal souls speak in these very places*).[4] Libraries deal with communications that attempt to defy place and period and, moreover, have spiritual qualities and overriding cultural values that transcend the means by which they are conveyed and preserved. Those cultural and spiritual qualities are inherent in any carrier of knowledge or means of communication, though they are more readily perceived in the familiar and the permanent.

The Role of the Library

The tasks of the library can be simply stated and understood. They are as true for a modern branch of a public library as they are for cathedral libraries of the Middle Ages or the great research collections of universities. Libraries exist to acquire, give access to, and safeguard carriers of knowledge and information in all forms and to provide instruction and assistance in the use of the collections to which their users have access. In short, libraries exist to give meaning to the continuing human attempt to transcend space and time in the advancement of knowledge and the preservation of culture. More than one hundred years ago, R. R. Bowker said the following:

> [It is for the librarian] . . . to classify and catalogue the records of ascertained knowledge, the literature of the whole past, and so bring the books to readers and the readers to books. He is the

---

3.   John Milton, *Areopagitica*. Santa Barbara: Bandanna Press, 1990.

4.   Quoted by Alfred Hessel in his *Geschichte der Bibliotheken*, translated, with supplementary material, by Reuben Peiss and published as *A history of libraries*, Washington: Scarecrow Press, 1950. Original source not found.

merchant, the middle man, of thought, and performs in this field the function which political economy recognizes as so important, of bringing goods to the place where they are wanted and so, also, creating demand. In this busy generation . . . the librarian makes time for his fellow mortals by saving it; for a minute saved is a minute added. And this function of organizing, of indexing, of time-saving and thought-saving, is associated peculiarly with the librarian of the nineteenth century.[5]

Allowing for our new means of communication and the likelihood that the librarian of today is a "she" rather than a "he," we can see in these words a perfect statement of what libraries and librarians do in the very late twentieth century.

Information and Knowledge

We are drowning in information but starved for knowledge.
John Naisbitt

Mortimer Adler has made a useful distinction between what he calls "the four goods of the mind."[6] Those four goods are **information**, **knowledge**, **understanding**, and **wisdom**. In defining each, Adler emphasizes that they are not equal, but "ascend in a scale of values, information having the least value, wisdom the greatest." Ours is a time in which the computer dominates and its speed is seen as its most valuable characteristic. It has been said that, when the only tool you have is a hammer, everything looks like a nail. It is understandable, therefore, that today the least valuable good—information— which also happens to be the most amenable to computerization, should be seen as the most central.

Proceeding from that premise, it is easy to see how discussion of the future of libraries should center on the digitizing of information and the use of computers to transfer information

---

5.   R. R. Bowker, "The work of the nineteenth-century librarian for the librarian of the twentieth," *Library Journal* 8 (September-October 1883), pp. 247–250.

6.   Mortimer Adler, *A guidebook to learning*, New York: Macmillan, 1986, pp. 110–134.

at great speed. On that basis, one can understand how unexamined labels such as "The Information Age" and unchallenged confusions such the "Virtual Library" should have gained such a hold on the popular imagination. It sometimes seems as though Gertrude Stein's observation that "everyone has so much information that they have lost their common sense"[7] has become literally true.

Adler treats information as a single good of the mind. In our opinion, information can be further subdivided into *data* (facts and other raw material that can be processed into useful information) and *information* (data processed and rendered useful). Each of these may exist independently—that is, they do not require the human mind to provide meaning and are, thus, peculiarly suitable for processing and transmission using electronic technology. As we move higher up the "ladder of learning," the human mind becomes vital and the role of the computer is consequently diminished. *Knowledge* can be defined as information transformed into meaning. It can be recorded and transmitted but the computer is by no means the ideal medium for such transmission. *Understanding* is knowledge integrated with a world view and a personal perspective and exists entirely within the human mind, as does *wisdom*, understanding made whole and generative.

Let us state, as strongly as we can, that libraries are **not wholly or even primarily about information**. They are about the preservation, dissemination, and use of recorded knowledge in whatever form it may come (see Figure 1) so that humankind may become more knowledgeable; through knowledge reach understanding; and, as an ultimate goal, achieve wisdom. The collection and absorption of data (discrete facts, numbers, etc.) and information (organized data) is often contextless and spasmodic. It may have a utilitarian purpose (usually brief) but has no enduring meaning unless the information so acquired is fitted into an intelligible structure of knowledge.

One may, for example, learn that Josephine Smith of Chico is five feet, six inches tall and that the average height of

---

7. Gertrude Stein, *Reflection on the atomic bomb,* ed. Robert Bartlett Haas, vol. 1 of *Uncollected writings of Gertrude Stein,* Los Angeles: Black Sparrow Press, 1973, p. 161.

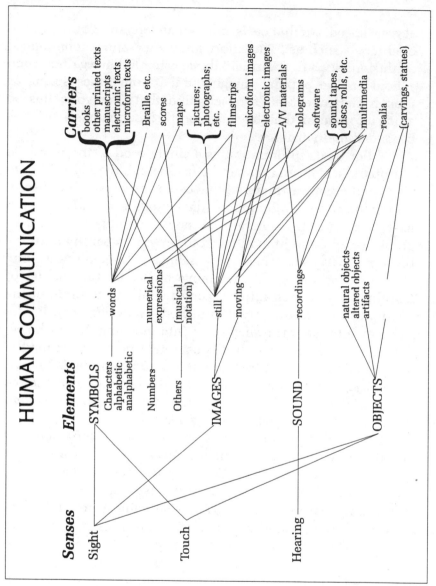

Figure 1. Human Communication

American females has increased by six inches in this century. That datum and that information have no meaning or interest beyond the trivial. The information may acquire interest if it is seen as a result of nutrition, improved public health, or other causality and fitted into an existing context of knowledge. Data and information, therefore, are building blocks for organized knowledge or they are nothing. This is no light point. If the only Adlerian "good" of the mind that can be sent down "the Information Superhighway" is the least important good, then we must look elsewhere for progress in and maintenance of our culture. Humans cannot live by information alone, and a society that is informed without being knowledgeable and wise will be a society of boorish conformity.

Laws of Library Science Revisited

More than sixty years ago, the great Indian librarian S. R. Ranganathan published his Five Laws of Library Science.[8] These brief statements remain, *mutatis mutandis*, as valid today as when they were promulgated. Ranganathan's Five Laws are:

- ◆ Books are for use.

- ◆ Books are for all; or, Every reader his book.

- ◆ Every book its reader.

- ◆ Save the time of the reader.

- ◆ A library is a growing organism.

When one looks beyond the language of 1931, one can see truths in these laws that are as applicable to the practice of librarianship today as they will be to the librarianship of tomorrow. In the process of thinking about the large issues addressed in this book, we have formulated Five New Laws of Library Science—a reinterpretation of Ranganathan's truths in the context of the library of today and its likely futures. We offer these laws in all humility, standing, as we do, on the shoulders of this giant of the library profession.

---

8.   S. R. Ranganathan, *Five laws of library science*, Madras: Madras Library Association; London: G. Blunt and Sons, 1931. (The laws themselves have been reprinted in numerous publications since.)

♦ Libraries serve humanity.

♦ Respect **all** forms by which knowledge is communicated.

♦ Use technology intelligently to enhance service.

♦ Protect free access to knowledge.

♦ Honor the past and create the future.

The new laws of library science are a framework within which libraries can survive and progress. They provide a tool enabling us to think about libraries and technology clearly and rationally.

Libraries Serve Humanity

The dominant ethic of librarianship is service. Libraries exist to serve the individual, community, and society as a whole. The word service connotes individual acts of help as well as the furtherance of the higher aspirations of humankind. Beyond that, service in librarianship implies an attention to quality, a desire to live up to and to surpass the expectations of library users. This law reminds us why we exist and urges us to consider any program or innovation in the light of service. The question "how will this change improve the service that this library gives?" is an analytical tool of great effectiveness. The urge to serve is at the root of successful careers in librarianship and its psychic rewards are many. In the words of Lee Finks: "It is, we should admit, a noble urge, this altruism of ours, one that seems both morally and psychologically good."[9]

Another aspect of this law is its emphasis on humanity, by which we mean the individual *and* humankind as a whole. Libraries do not exist to serve exclusivist groups (though on occasion their sources of funding may make this seem to be true). Our true mission is both to the individual seeker of truth and to the wider goals and aspirations of the culture.

---

9.   Lee W. Finks, "Values without shame," *American Libraries*, April 1989, pp. 352–356.

Respect All Forms by Which Knowledge Is Communicated

In the early chapters of this book, we deal with the myths and realities that surround electronic technology with a continuing hysteria about "the death of the book," "the paperless society," and other dreams and nightmares. We hope to demonstrate that the truth of the matter lies in respecting all forms of communication for the strengths that each brings to the conquest of space and time; in acknowledging that the library of the future will use all kinds of carriers of knowledge and information; and in studying the realities of each means of communication in the light of the history of innovation in communication.

The plain fact is that each new means of communication enhances and supplements the strengths of all previous means. Moreover, this appears to be an ineluctable process. This is despite the fact that each new means is greeted with predictions that it will eliminate previous forms of communication. Here is Robert Benchley writing in 1928 on the advent of the talkies:

> The movietone is a big success in the hinterland . . . One theatre man we heard talking about it said that, being a mechanical thing, it would unquestionably be perfected and . . . mean a revolution in the amusement field. He said half the legitimate theatres in New York will be out of business as such within ten years.[10]

We do not advocate clinging to print-on-paper, images on film, or grooves on discs in cases when newer technology clearly offers better alternatives. Equally, we do not advocate replacing print-on-paper, etc., when new technology is less effective, more costly, or has other disadvantages. We believe very strongly that the best approach to the future of libraries lies in this utilitarianism. Furthermore, it is surely more affirming and positive to see each advance in communication as enriching and enhancing the universe of knowledge rather than to see it as narrowing and destroying choices.

---

10. [Robert Benchley], "The coming of the movietone," *New Yorker*, July 14, 1928, pp. 16–17.

Use Technology Intelligently to Enhance Service

A false dichotomy has been created in the minds of many librarians. It is almost as though one has to pick between two sides, each of which is violently opposed to the other. In reality, one does not have to choose between being a Luddite and a soulless technocrat.

The history of progress in librarianship has been a story of the successful integration of new technologies and new means of communication into existing programs and services. Librarians have welcomed innovation and have, if anything, been sometimes overeager in the embrace of the new. The *intelligent* use of technology involves:

♦ seeking answers to problems rather than seeking applications of interesting new technology;

♦ weighing the cost-effectiveness, cost-benefit, and, above all, impact on service of any proposed innovation;

♦ rethinking the program, service, or workflow that is being automated rather than automating what one has.

Online catalogues are demonstrably superior to card and microform catalogues. Networked indexing and abstracting services are demonstrably superior to their print forerunners. It goes without saying that modern libraries should have electronic circulation systems and acquisitions and serial control systems and should provide access, by one means or another, to the world of digitized data and facts of all kinds (numeric, bibliographic, image-based, and textual

Looked at objectively, the relative roles of electronic communication and non-electronic communication (print, sound recordings, film/video, etc.) become clear. Electronic methods are best for "housekeeping" and for giving access to data and small, discrete packets of textual, numeric, and visual information (such as those found in many reference works). Each of the other media has areas in which it is the best. In particular, print-on-paper is and will be the preeminent medium for the communication of cumulative knowledge (for a detailed examination of this matter, see Chapter 2).

Protect Free Access to Knowledge

Two of the professional values advanced by Lee Finks are **stewardship** and **democratic values**. The former calls upon us to "take responsibility for the library as an institution." In Finks' eloquent words:

> The library and its fruits must exist 50 years from now, indeed a thousand years from now, for us to have fulfilled our mission. This, in essence, is Jesse Shera's notion of social epistemology, our concern with searching out and assuring the safe passage onward in time of that part of the "social transcript" that is worthy of standing as part of the library. If we don't do this, the culture of the present and past will be lost, which is a prospect that we cannot accept.[11]

People of the future will know only that which we preserve. This is a weighty responsibility and one that should be in the minds of all librarians. Our praiseworthy pursuit of the preservation of intellectual freedom for today's materials should, of course, be continued. However, it should be noted that allowing the records of the past to disappear is a kind of censorship. Libraries are the collective archive of human achievement and the knowledge of the ages. This important role must be at the forefront of any consideration of technological change.

Libraries are central to freedom—social, political, and intellectual freedom. We believe in universal education and trust in the wisdom of an informed and knowledgeable citizenry. It is scarcely exaggerated to say that a truly free society without libraries freely available to all is an oxymoron. A society without uncensored libraries is a society open to tyranny. In our view, libraries must preserve *all* records of all societies and communities and make those records available to all. Putting an emphasis on the speedy delivery of ephemeral "information" to the detriment of knowledge would be a betrayal of that trust.

---

11. Lee W. Finks, op. cit.

Honor the Past and Create the Future

We live in an ahistorical age. The little that is known about the past is not used to inform the actions of the present. Anyone can see the bad effects on society, politics, and daily life of ignoring Santayana's famous dictum:

> Progress, far from consisting in change, depends on retentiveness. When change is absolute there remains no being to improve and no direction is set for possible improvement; and when experience is not retained . . . infancy is perpetual. Those who cannot remember the past are condemned to repeat it.[12]

We do not advocate clinging to old things because they are old, nor do we advocate discarding old things because they are old. The library of tomorrow must be one that retains not only the best of the past but also a sense of the history of libraries and of human communication. Without that, the library will be purely reactive, a thing of the moment, sometimes useful and sometimes not but never central to human society. With a sense of history and the knowledge of enduring values and the continuity of our mission, the library can never be destroyed. Along with this sense of time future being contained in time past,[13] there must be the acceptance of the challenge of innovation. It is neither the easiest of prescriptions nor the most fashionable, but libraries need to combine the past and the future in a rational, clear-headed, unsentimental manner. The chapters that follow are intended to show the practical implications of that approach and to constitute a survival guide for all those who value libraries.

---

12. George Santayana, *The life of reason*, 2nd ed., Vol. 1, New York: Scribner, 1927, p. 284.

13. "Time present and time past/Are both perhaps present in time future,/ And time future contained in time past." T. S. Eliot, "Four quartets," *Burnt norton*, London: Faber, 1944, p. 7.

2

The Life of Print

All the jumbled voices flying through the air—the video voices and the music voices, the computer-message voices and the talk-radio voices—all the voices that, we are told, are destined to drown out the quiet voices of books. But a book, amid the din of the new and insistent voices, can be the strongest clearest voice of all. A book—one voice on a printed page, speaking intimately and persuasively to one person who is listening to that voice on a timetable of his or her own choosing.

Bob Greene

The debate about the future of print is really not about print-on-paper versus electronic technology (after all most print-on-paper is the result of computer technology). It is about reading and the best means to read. To state a simple, central theme of this book: Reading is important to the individual and to society, and print-on-paper is best for sustained reading leading to the acquisition of knowledge.

In all the debate and confusion, there is a broad measure of agreement that reading is good, that literacy matters, and that those who do not (or cannot) read are at a severe societal disadvantage. There is not broad agreement on the value of print-on-paper in the form of books and printed journals when it comes to transmitting knowledge. Without anyone raising an eyebrow at his reductionism, a well-known library educator and writer can write:

> There is nothing wrong with books, but there is nothing particularly right with them either. They are part of an ever-changing and evolving array of information formats, and we have to remember that the printed book as we know it occupies only a very short span of our profession. When a child is handed his or her first disk or fiche, I hope it is by the children's librarian. [1]

It is absurd to claim that books *per se* are irrelevant or part of an "ever-changing and evolving array of information formats." Both the premise and the conclusion are patently false, but the assertions go unchallenged. Why? We believe it is because, though librarians emphasize the importance of literacy, they think of it as being concerned with the acquisition of functional skills by the disadvantaged. Moreover, in terror of being considered out of date, many librarians have tacitly agreed on the false egalitarianism that does not allow a qualitative distinction between, say, reading *War and Peace* and watching MTV. Sustained reading leading to the acquisition of knowledge *is* important and *is* good for the individual and for society. We wish to demonstrate that print-on-paper (the "book") is the best vehicle for sustained reading and is likely to remain so for the foreseeable future.

The Health of Print

Print is not dead. Print is not dying. Print is not even vaguely ill. Despite the best efforts of those who predict (and have predicted for many years) that print-on-paper is due to be replaced in the near future, there are no objective reasons to believe that this is so. On the contrary, there are signs that more enlightened futurists have come to more sensible conclusions.

---

1.   Herbert S. White, "What do we want to be when we grow up?" *Library Journal* 119 (May 15, 1994), pp. 50–51.

Paper is completely random-access; it's high resolution; it's portable; it's almost interactive in the way it gives you the ability to determine the pace, to go backward or forward. Paper is still the best way of delivering high thought content.[2]

Typically, those who would like print to die make wildly mistaken assumptions about the economics of print, ignore or deny the advantages of print, and otherwise distort or ignore the facts in order to reach their conclusions. Common sense demands that we pay attention to the real world market of print-on-paper, the real advantages of that medium, and realistic economic issues.

Print: The Real Numbers

Listening to all-electronic advocates, the reader is likely to believe that books, magazines, and newspapers are gasping their last dying breaths. Raymond Kurzweil[3] appears to be back-pedaling on some of his forecasts but still maintains that "the day of fully viable virtual books is not far off" and "it has become accepted that computerized books [sic] are *better* than the paper variety in certain categories."[4] It turns out that he is talking about reference works and other containers of data and information and is ignoring the issue of sustained reading.

The doomsayers always use the tired cliché of the buggy-whip industry—the one that was, allegedly, killed by the automobile. Publishers, librarians, and readers are seen as an aggregation of sentimentalists resisting the inevitability of progress. In some futurists' view the print-on-paper industries are fading away and should be gone in another couple of years: a vivid projection that has the disadvantage of being untrue. Here are some facts to counter the Death-of-the-Book theory.

---

2.   Louis Rosetto (editor of *Wired*), quoted by Horace Bent in *Bookseller*, July 30, 1993.

3.   Author of a series of columns under the rubric "Futurecast" in *Library Journal*.

4.   Raymond Kurzweil, "The virtual book revisited," *Library Journal* 188 (February 15, 1993), pp. 145–146.

♦ Book sales in the United States increased almost 16 percent in the first nine months of 1992 as compared to 1991. That is real growth, in excess of inflation.

♦ Between April 1991 and March 1992, 822 million adult books were sold in the United States. That is 7 percent more adult books than were sold in the equivalent period a year previously. It is also roughly eight books per household, and at least one book was purchased in two-thirds of all households. These numbers do not include the vast and expanding children and juvenile book market.

♦ The entire publishing/printing industry represents more than $100 billion in the United States, and the industry continues to grow. Book publishing in the U.S., including adult and juvenile books, accounted for about $21 billion in sales in 1992.

♦ Periodical publishing as a whole, including magazines and newspapers, is more than a $53 billion field in the United States. Note that most revenue for magazines and newspapers comes from advertising ($37 billion) rather than from subscriptions and purchases.

♦ Public library book circulation also continues to grow, by 15 percent from 1990 to 1991.[5]

Throughout the twentieth century, librarians have joined others in suggesting that some new medium would sweep away print—but, in the past, such suggestions always came while public library circulation was declining.[6] While those suggestions of total displacement—whether by phonograph, radio,

5.   The figures in this section are taken from, and footnoted in, Kathleen de la Peña McCook's fine article "The first virtual reality" in the July/August 1993 *American Libraries*, apart from those relating to sales and receipts in publishing, which were derived from U.S. Census and McCann-Erickson, Inc. reports.

6.   These fears of replacement are well documented in Klaus Mussman's *Technological innovations in libraries, 1860–1960: an anecdotal history*, Westport, Conn: Greenwood Press, 1993.

television or other diversions, real and imaginary—have always been wrong, at least there were plausible numbers to back up the predictions. That is by no means the case today.

One important delusion is that the electronic revolution has created a new source of data that was previously available only in books and magazines. It has been a good many years since most data was available in books and magazines, if indeed it ever was. Most data is meaningless outside its local sphere, and most will never become widely useful information. When someone says print is dying, they are either ignorant, using misleading statistical comparisons, or deliberately misstating the situation. Print is *not* dying, and will not die as long as there is an open marketplace.

Individual magazines do die. They always have and always will. They are always supplanted by new titles. New magazines are springing up rapidly and some of them are incredibly successful. Indeed, the most striking voice of the multimedia electronic-everything field is a print magazine called *Wired*. The avant-garde creators of this publication tried to publish it in electronic form but soon came to the conclusion that the best way to do what they needed to do was with ink on paper.

Meanwhile, *PC Magazine*, a specialized periodical that is bulky enough to frighten off the casual reader, circulates more than a million paid copies 22 times a year—and both *PC/Computing* and *PC World* circulate only slightly less than a million. There are magazines of all kinds on bookstores and supermarket shelves and in the mail every day—magazines with astonishingly high production values and great appeal to specialist markets and the general public. Not only is there no evidence of a decline in the magazine market; there is considerable evidence that the market is competitive, productive, innovative, and flourishing.

Reading: Still Best on Paper

One of the sillier forecasts of an all-electronic future is the idea that everyone will read from computer devices. Such a thing may not be impossible, but it is implausible for a number of reasons. The facts are that books work and they work better than any alternative for *sustained reading*. While computer devices are better for communicating data and small packets of information, even most technologically knowledgeable people who do not have their own axes to grind and who still take time for reading confirm the obvious: for linear text of more than a few paragraphs, print on paper is the preferred medium.

Print-on-paper is also the best available medium for high-resolution reproduction of graphics. To take just one example, significant for both price and quality, Abbeville's *Treasures of the Uffizi* offers 275 full-color illustrations in an $11.95 "tiny folio" paperback.[7] It is a good representation of the continuing strength of print even in cases in which text is not a primary issue. A $20 CD-ROM can include many more illustrations, but not with the detail and depth of full-color printing. Alternatively, that CD-ROM can include very nearly the detail and depth of good full-color printing, but only in the Kodak Photo CD format, limited to 100 photographs per disc.

Appropriate Technology: Books Work

Books are the result of a highly refined technology—printing—developed over several hundred years and made more cost-effective and timely by today's computer technology. Books are not only appropriate and the best bargain in many cases but are also the superior means of communicating knowledge and large accumulations of information meant to be read in a linear fashion. Books should, and almost certainly will, survive and prosper for precisely those reasons.

Even those who assume that many or most periodical publications will migrate to electronic form may draw the line at books, particularly books filled with narrative text (nearly all fiction and most nonreference nonfiction). As Allan Kornblum commented in a speech at the Library of Congress:

> Books that are both public and intimate—the kind that are read in the bathroom or on the beach, in the subway or on the sofa—those books will not all go to modem. Good books are not

7.   Caterina Caneva, *Treasures of the Uffizi,* New York: Abbeville Press, 1994.

the stuff of fly-by-night technology. They fit our hands, our brains and bodies, and we'll continue to insist that they do.[8]

Today and for the foreseeable future, no electronic medium can begin to compare with ink on paper for readability, even if we discount the aesthetic pleasure of the book or magazine itself as a factor. The problems of readability are not being solved and there is reason to doubt that some of them may be solvable. We will address three of those problems briefly: *light, resolution,* and *speed of reading.*

Light

Virtually every readable electronic display uses transmitted light—light shining in your face as you read—which is inherently more tiring than the reflected light used for book reading. Displays using only reflected light appear to be at a dead end; for one thing, the contrast they provide is nowhere near high enough. Inevitably, a reader of a transmitted-light text will stop reading sooner; will read more slowly; and will get more headaches. The reader will turn from a transmitted-light to a reflected-light medium with an audible sigh of relief.

Resolution

Electronic displays resolve at between 72 and 101 dots per inch—some a little higher, cheap ones a little lower. Most high-quality VGA displays actually have 90 to 97 picture elements per inch; the triads of phosphor dots are spaced 0.26 or 0.28 mm apart, and there are 25.4 mm to an inch. The densest displays available (other than in a few specialized markets) use Trinitron tubes that have phosphor lines spaced 0.25 mm apart, leading, in theory, to a maximum of 101 picture elements per inch. Both of these are theoretical maxima that assume that the electron guns can focus absolutely precisely at all locations and at all times.

In reality, most displays cannot be used at their highest resolution, because most software is not designed to take proper advantage of that resolution. Most modern personal computer users are likely to see resolutions of 72 to 75 dots per inch. The

---

8.   *LC Information Bulletin,* December 13, 1993, p. 466.

original Macintosh, the first personal computer with identical horizontal and vertical resolution, had a 72-dot-per-inch display; for a modern PC or Macintosh, 800-by-600 Super VGA displayed on a 15-inch monitor is roughly 75 dots per inch.

The lowest resolution of printed text in everyday publishing is between 300 and 600 dots per inch—the resolution of ink-jet and laser printers. Many magazines and books are prepared from imagesetters resolving at 1,200 to 2,400 lines per inch. Thus, books, magazines, and most other printed documents typically have from *16 to 1,200 times* as many elements per square inch than screens. Three hundred dots per inch is 16 times the print density of 75 dots per inch, not four; there are 90,000 dots per square inch as compared to 5,625.

The result? 10-point type is easily read on the page, and 8-point type is not too difficult for those with normal eyesight. On the screen, the reader will squint at 10 points, and 8 points is almost hopeless. Usually, what is seen as 10-point type on the screen is actually enlarged at least 20 to 40 percent from actual size.

These are all problems of the cathode ray tube (CRT) screen. It appears that non-CRT displays are not the answer, at least not those based on any known technology. Affordable liquid crystal displays (LCDs) resolve at no more than 80 dots per inch, and there are enormous technological difficulties in creating affordable, bright LCD displays much larger than 11 inches. Those who imagine a world in which lengthy texts could only be read from the screen tend to resort to hand-waving when confronted with the resolution factor, rarely referring to any real-world devices that solve the problem. Some have even made the baseless assertion that computer displays already offer resolution equivalent to paperback books.

Here is a simple test available to anyone owning a personal computer running Macintosh System 7, Windows 3.x, or some equivalent graphical interface. Key in some text from a book, a magazine, or a newspaper, setting margins so that line breaks are the same as in the printed material. Use a typeface that is as close as possible to the printed page—e.g., for newspapers, Times New Roman or another Times variant will probably do. Now, adjust the size of the displayed type until it is as comfortable to read, at the same distance, as the printed type—or, to make it tougher, until it is both as comfortable to read and has the same quality.

It is quite likely that the reader will need more than twice the area to get newspaper text to be as readable, and at least four times the area (that is, twice the height and width) to make even low-quality book or magazine text as readable on the screen as on the page. Even then, the type will not be as easy on the eyes. The reader sees the dots, subliminally at least, when reading text on the screen. The mind is doing extra work to resolve those dots into characters and words.

Speed and Comprehension

Light and resolution are problems that affect the speed at which one can read; so does area. One can normally see only about half to a third of a print book page on a screen, even at the degraded resolution of the screen. For magazines with relatively small body text, the figures are even worse. Some estimates are that reading from a screen is about 30 percent slower than reading from a printed page, but that is probably only true for difficult factual material that needs to be read word for word. If a reader is skimming or browsing or reading light fiction, there is no comparison at all—reading from the page will be several times faster than reading from the screen. To be sure, there are many cases in which the screen will be much faster than the printed page—not for reading, but for getting to the short passages to be read for specific informational purposes.

Consider the most degraded print with which most people deal—the daily newspaper, printed at high speeds on low-grade paper. Given a 15-inch display and with the text set for comfortable reading, it is most likely that there will be less than one eighth of a newspaper page on a screen. Thus, to do the equivalent of a five-second scan of a front page, the screen must be rewritten at least eight times. Not surprisingly, "newspapers" designed for electronic transmission and to be read from the screen have not proven to be popular.

Most writers and editors have learned that editing requires hard copy because the editor does not see as much in the text when it is read on a screen. That seems counter-intuitive, given that it takes longer to read copy from the screen. It is likely that the extra mental effort involved in reading from a screen dis-

tracts the editor from the task of focusing on sentence structure
and the like. Edward J. Valauskas puts it this way:

> Distracted by the monitor's construction of text on the screen,
> we often don't spot errors literally right in front of our eyes. All
> of us have learned to print all of our word processing on paper
> before shipping it off electronically. Indeed, paper contributes
> to the health of our writing.[9]

There are other problems with computers as replacements for
printed media. Even the best notebook computers are vastly less
convenient than paperback books and mass-market magazines
for reading on the fly, during odd moments and in odd locations—and notebook computers require batteries, representing
an additional cost and ecological problem in an area of technology that does not promise rapid improvement. Even technology journalists find online reading unsatisfying, unless they
are ideologically committed to doing everything electronically,
no matter how inefficient it may be.

Usability: Print for Long Texts

The point we are making is not that the technology is lagging
and that we should all just wait for a few years for all these
problems to be solved. Some of them may be. Others will not.
The point is that we have a first-rate medium for extended
reading—it is called print-on-paper. In a real sense, those who
advance electronic media for sustained reading are hawking a
flawed solution to a non-existent problem. At the very most,
until electronic media perform at least as well as print on paper
in every aspect of readability, there is really no reason to
hypothesize the replacement of nonreference, widely circulated print material. Why should we spend time and money
searching for an alternative to something that works well?
Death-of-the-Book advocates are alchemists in hot pursuit of an
illusion in a world of real scientists making genuine advances.

---

9.   Edward J. Valauskas, "Paper-based or digital text: what's best?"
Computers in Libraries 14 (January 1994), p. 45.

Hypertext and Linear Text

Some futurists assert that making text accessible at the paragraph level, with user-defined links to other paragraphs, inherently makes the text more worthwhile. Serious prose writers and serious readers will disagree. Here are the words of one writer (who happens to be a technophile) on the topic of hypertext as a substitute for books:

> I will not be browsed through. The essence of writing books is the author's right to tell the story in his own words and in the order he chooses. Hypertext . . . completely eliminates what I perceive as my value added, turns this exercise into something like the Yellow Pages, and totally eliminates the prospect that it will help fund my retirement.[10]

Order and cumulative exposition are significant to well-written linear text that seeks to impart knowledge. Paragraphs in substantial books have meaning only in the context of what precedes and follows them. In addition, hypertext is not free-text searching—it requires that links be established—and a hypertext limits the reader to the links that someone has prepared. If that person is the author, then the author's job has become much larger while the text itself is, paradoxically, diminished. Not only must text be cut down to bite-size chunks, but the author must prepare multiple sequences, presumably with some sense that they will all be readable.

Small wonder that most authors show little enthusiasm for hypertext. Most authors are serious about taking or creating knowledge and imposing form and shape on that knowledge so that *their* vision is presented to the reader—not a vision that will arise from serendipity or, more likely, will not arise at all.

If the creator of the hypertext version is someone other than the author of the original text, that person is assuming a new level of editorial intrusion, one that raises significant questions. A few writers and some readers fail to appreciate the virtues of

---

10. Robert X. Cringely, *Accidental empires: how the boys of Silicon Valley make their millions, battle foreign competition, and still can't get a date*, Reading, Mass.: Addison-Wesley, 1992; New York: HarperBusiness, 1993, p. 69.

the cumulative presentation of knowledge that linear text affords. Paragraph-level access makes development of complex arguments impossible. The author has no chance to build understanding in the reader. There are, to be sure, cases in which the virtues of linear text are overshadowed by paragraph-level access. Such exceptions are texts that do not aim to present a coherent argument or a global picture of their subject that rises beyond the purely factual.

One writer asserted that a good way to choose a book in order to learn a new subject is to open it to page 14, page 54, and page 140. If the reader cannot make sense of each of these random pages, the book is too complex. The proponent of this theory has spectacularly missed the function of good linear texts intended to impart knowledge. By the time a reader has read pages 1 to 140, he or she should understand the subject much better than when on page 14. Indeed, if a book is designed to inform on a subject that is new to the reader, that reader has every right to be suspicious if all of, say, page 154 is instantly accessible. What is the point of reading the text in that case?

We must draw a distinction between linear text translated into hypertext and the creative use of original hypertext applications. The latter can be enormously useful. Currently, the most widespread use of hypertext may be the Windows Help system designed to provide online help for Windows-based software. A good Windows Help module can include the equivalent of several volumes of documentation. A good Windows Help system makes it possible for an informed user to make advanced use of a program without ever opening the print manual, and hypertext links (combined with the searchable index, expandable table of contents, and clear backtracking capability that are part of Windows Help) provide a good deal of that value. Hypertext can be similarly valuable for many forms of quick reference and immediate instruction. Good hypertext is not the same as good linear text, and may require even more thought to prepare. At the same time, converting good linear text to hypertext will, typically, be less satisfactory than either by itself.

Publishers: Not Just Printers

Another claim of some futurists, particularly in the context of the imagined omnipresent Information Superhighway (the I-way), is that the I-way will stimulate scholarship and discussion by making us all publishers. Anyone with anything to say will be able to publish it just as effectively as anyone else; those terrible publishers will not be able to restrict the flow of worthwhile material, and we will not have to pay for their role as printers and distributors. The same is supposedly true for journals—everyone will post articles as they are written, thus eliminating all this nonsense with scholarly journals that, among other sins, delay publication by so long.

For those already on the Internet, the common-sense response is simple—think of what the Internet user encounters every day. Then think of what can be read in journals and books from serious and respected publishers. The contrast between random accumulations of opinion, disconnected data, unverified assertions, and contextless statements on the one hand and ordered, cumulative, authoritative presentations of knowledge and organized information on the other should make anyone think twice about the desirability of eliminating book publishers and the traditional journal process.

Publishers are not just printers and distributors. As noted later in this chapter, only 10 to 14 percent of the price of a typical trade book can be attributed to printing and distributing the physical artifact—the book. Between 80 and 90 cents of every dollar spent on books by individuals and libraries goes not only for publicity and profit, but also to development, editing, and other filtering and gatekeeping functions. Gatekeeping is an even more important function of the better scholarly journals.

Given the speed and efficiency of contemporary publication techniques, the lag between article completion and publication is due far more to those gatekeeping requirements than to production and distribution delays. There is already casual evidence that refereed electronic journals can take *longer* to publish material than some refereed print journals. That is scarcely surprising, given variations in refereeing efficiency and the time people are willing to devote to editorial duties for what are still seen as "fringe" publications.

It is hard to believe that we would be better off without editing, without peer review, and without the authority bestowed by respected publishers and journals to suggest which papers or books deserve closest attention. It should be clear to any Internet user, even those who read library-related lists, that there is no comparison between the quality of what appears there and that of a good journal, periodical or book. Only the willful would deny that publishers add crucial value to the texts they publish.

Economics of Print

Some writers have said that print is doomed for economic reasons. Let us look a little closer. One of the false assumptions behind these forecasts is that book readership is *already* declining. As we have noted, it is not. With few exceptions, the numbers of books published and sold in the United States has increased each year for many years.

Another bogus comparison is that between the *actual cost* of electronic distribution in a free Internet environment and the *list price* of commercial print products. This is no comparison at all, since editorial and other operations are not included in the electronic costs, while, of course, the list price of a book includes all aspects of publishing. Any rational discussion of the economics of print and electronic publishing must begin with the factual comparison of like with like, including the substantial hidden costs of electronic publishing.

It is not helpful to treat print publishing as a monolithic entity. Publishing is made up of a large number of niches, markets, and categories. We will consider some aspects of current print publishing, beginning with a category that should be replaced by electronic publishing and distribution.

Short-Lived Reference Works

Abstracts and indexes may be the best examples of texts that never made much sense as books. In printed form they are too bulky; distribution and printing represent an unreasonable overhead; they are inherently slow to produce; and they are user-unfriendly. Replacing such print products with CD-ROMs does not, in any real way, take us toward the "virtual library." CD-ROMs are, fundamentally, just big, hard-to-read but easy-to-search texts in little packages; they are published items that libraries buy and house, and to which they provide access.

Libraries must ensure, when these publications are only available in electronic form, that back issues of abstracts and indexes continue to be available. Electronic indexes and abstracts can be much more powerful than print publications, but they still pose some problems. Finding specific items appears to be easier online or on CD-ROM, but understanding the scope of the reference work can be much more difficult. What is really available online or on that disc? How does the user gain a quick overview of the whole?

Theoretically, short-run short-lived reference works, particularly those that are bulky in print, should be cheaper in electronic form. There is no evidence that these savings are occurring. As librarians, we should ask why this is so. Even though the real potential for savings is much less than many expect—since the bulk of costs for most reference works is still incurred in preparing, editing, and organizing the text—there is no question that a 2,000-page work can be produced much less expensively on CD-ROM than in paper. The savings may only be $20 or $30 (more for short-run works), but that is still a savings, one that should be passed on to the buyer.

There are, of course, other costs to the library that are associated with electronic reference works. Online resources require terminals or workstations. CD-ROM publications require computers and, increasingly, networking. The user needs more than a table and a good light to use an electronic index. Nevertheless, many reference products make more sense in electronic form than in paper form, and we should expect to see more such publishing in the future.

Short-Run Monographs and Journals

The next-clearest case for electronics replacing print on paper is that of short-run materials: scholarly monographs and journals that are published in editions of a few hundred. In such cases, the cost of producing a print edition can be considerable on a per-copy basis, particularly if the materials are bulky or require color or other special considerations. While book printing is remarkably inexpensive at even moderate volumes, the startup costs are high, as is also true for CD-ROM production.

The cost of printing and production is not the only issue, however. Short-run monographs and journals are poor candidates for electronic *publication* as such, unless many mono graphs or journal issues can be combined into single archival CD-ROMs. That could work economically, although it would work against timely distribution. For materials unlikely to be needed very often, archival scholarly publishing in digital form may make economic sense and can offer great economy of storage for libraries.

The more feasible alternative for short-run items needed in a timely manner is electronic distribution—making them available over electronic networks. At the moment, that method still poses thorny problems of usability, authority, copyright, and the balance between access and payment, but these problems may be resolved in this specialized context long before they are resolved for general publications.

Trade and Medium-Run Books

Consider ordinary books—novels, nonfiction books, the stuff of public libraries and liberal arts and sciences collections— and specialized books that sell more than 1,000 copies. We already know there are good reasons why people prefer these texts (with or without graphics) in printed form, and that this preference is likely to mean that print-on-paper will be a part of life for the foreseeable future. Let us consider the economics of books.

Electronic publishing is said to be much cheaper than print publishing. This is almost a cliché, but one that lacks the saving grace of most clichés—that they are true. When looked at objectively, this statement is hard to sustain. Quite apart from the real costs of electronic storage and networking mechanisms themselves, not even a significant minority of the cost of printed books and journals lies in printing and distributing those materials.

Print publishing involves several costs, which vary depending on the types of material being published. Books involve salary costs for acquisitions editors, copy editors, production editors, layout people, artists, indexers, and proofreaders. They also require expenditures for typesetting or imagesetting, platemaking and printing, binding, distribution, and publicity. There is also the important matter of profit, not to mention the overhead of management, offices for editors, equipment, and years of editorial development for many books.

In the case of many publications, the typesetting and imagesetting costs have already been reduced or eliminated, as have some proofreading costs. This book, for example, went directly from Walt Crawford's laser printer to the printer. There were no typesetting costs; one entire proofreading cycle was eliminated; and the layout costs were relatively minor.

Electronic publishing eliminates expenditures for imagesetting, printing, binding, and some portion of distribution. It has no effect on the need to acquire, edit, design (for best reading), index (or create hypertext links), and publicize the publication; it does not reduce a publishing house's overhead. There is still a distribution cost, even if it's hidden; for CD-ROM, there are both a "printing" and a distribution cost.

The one area in which electronic publications are economically superior to printed publications is the cost of physical production and (for the moment, at least) distribution. To understand the financial comparison, it is necessary to know the proportion of the price of a book that is due to production and distribution costs. That will vary, of course, depending on the print run, the form of binding, nature of illustrations, etc. A plausible estimate of the cost of production and distribution of typical medium-run hardbound books is 10 to 14 percent of the price. Oxford University Press says that 30 percent of expenses for a not-for-profit publisher are production costs, but that excludes profit margin and is for short-run, traditionally typeset monographs.[11]

---

11. "Where does the money go (and where does it come from)?" *CLR Reports*, new series (January 1994), pp. 1–2.

There it is—the potential savings under optimum conditions is $1 to, at most, $3 of every $10 of book price. The book costs typically include typesetting and a growing number of books do not incur typesetting charges. "Quality" paperbacks cost about $2 a copy to print and distribute. Even for a 300-page hardbound permanent-paper book, setting aside typesetting charges, the cost of physical production for a 1,000-copy run is unlikely to be much more than $4 to $6 per copy. For a 1,000-copy CD-ROM, the cost of production would typically be about $2.50 per copy. Thus, the potential savings is $1.50 to $4.50 per copy at best.

The bottom line is this: for run-of-the-mill trade and specialty books, anything with at least 1,000 to 1,500 probable sales, traditional publishing makes economic sense—and electronic publishing does not offer major savings.

Mass-Market Paperbacks: The True Revolution

When it comes to mass-market paperbacks, the numbers are dramatically different and favor print even more directly. Using high-speed presses and paper that is not much better than newsprint, mass-market paperbacks are so cheap to produce that publishers cannot be bothered to take unsold returns. Instead, merchants just tear off the covers and ship them back for credit. With luck, what remains of the book is recycled.

Production costs per copy of a mass-market paperback are almost certainly well under a dollar, and probably less than fifty cents: considerably less than a CD-ROM, and probably less than any plausible means of electronic communication. Mass-market paperbacks represent the true information revolution. They may not be beautiful, but they are readable and cheap, they are everywhere, and they keep people reading.

The Curious Economics of Mass-Market Magazines

What about mass-market magazines—for example, anything likely to be found in a supermarket magazine rack? Such magazines may have as little as 50,000 circulation, but quite a few have circulations in the millions. Are they candidates for displacement by electronic means? Not in any future that makes sense. Subscribers and casual purchasers really do not pay most of the cost of most mass-market magazines; advertisers do. They pay those costs because they know who buys the magazines and know that print advertising works—partly because the life of the advertisement is as long as the life of the magazine issue. That also holds true for many magazines that do not appear on newsstands, including the extreme cases, the many "controlled-circulation" magazines and newspapers whose subscribers pay nothing at all for them.

PC Magazine costs about $30 per year for 22 issues ($1.40 each) averaging 500 pages each and clearly represents the efforts of a large and expert editorial staff. It probably costs half the issue price just to mail the monster. Most of the editorial and production money (including the publisher's profit) comes from the advertisers. Would it make sense to convert *PC Magazine* to electronic form? How could an electronic version be as readable and handsome and why would readers look at the advertisements? In fact, the publisher (Ziff-Davis) is experimenting with a CD-ROM "version" of *PC Magazine*, but as a quarterly supplement and at a much higher per-issue price ($15 to $20, including postage, per issue). Portions of *PC Magazine* are available online, using Ziff-Davis's ZiffNet on CompuServe. The user must, of course, pay CompuServe's rates. After all, there is no such thing as free information. The text (but not the advertisements or graphics) is available on CD-ROM in *Computer Select*, after some delay, at $495 to $995 a year.

More than 100,000 people who influence corporate computer purchases get another Ziff-Davis publication every week. It is called *PC Week* and contains around 120 pages of nicely produced matter in a tabloid format. It costs these subscribers nothing because advertisers pick up the tab. Many parts of the country have free local computer monthlies—the San Francisco area has a 300-page monthly and a 200-page fortnightly, both free. How can electronics beat those prices? Let us take a completely different example—*Consumer Reports*. It carries no advertising and, consequently, is not cheap—about $1.50 a month, for a relatively slender magazine of about 80 pages. However, those pages contain only editorial material; it represents millions of dollars worth of testing; and it includes loads of photographs and tables. Could this be done as effectively and

more cheaply using electronic methods? Almost certainly not—
and very few readers would be willing to read entire issues of
Consumer Reports on Prodigy.

Magazines cover such a broad range that few sweeping
statements make sense. As one example of print efficiency,
however, if editorial costs are eliminated (by using volunteer
editors and referees), typesetting and production costs are
minimized (by using desktop publishing techniques), the best
professional printing on permanent paper is used, and the
magazine is distributed by professional distribution services, a
120-page quarterly 6-by-9-inch journal with a subscription list
of 6,000 can be produced and distributed for less than $10 a
subscriber *per year*, not including the costs of billing subscribers but also not including any offset from advertising revenues.

Newspapers: The Social Context

Futurists tell us that electronic publishing will bring us better
newspapers. Specifically, we will have personalized newspapers—newspapers that contain all the stories that we care
about, and only those stories. Moreover, these electronic newspapers will be far more up-to-date than the big city newspapers
of today. *PC Magazine* calls such papers *The Daily Me*.[12] Such
papers probably seem desirable to some people and, if they
have enough money, they can actually get something along
these lines. Right now, that "something" will probably be from
5 to 40 screens of information (the equivalent of up to five
newspaper pages) for anything from $1 to $5 per day (3 to 15
times the price of a daily newspaper).

The Daily Me may appeal to some but, in our opinion, is a
disastrous development, from an economic perspective and
from a social perspective. The economics are pretty straightforward. If it is a personalized paper, it probably cannot be paid
for by advertising revenues, so there will be an hourly charge
or a charge per item. Reading online is slow and laborious. If
the *Me* reader downloads, there will be a charge for that. Even
if the charge is as low as $12 an hour, how much news could
be read for the price of a daily newspaper? The equivalent of a

---

12. See, for example, *PC Magazine* 12, no. 15 (September 14, 1993), p. 29.

front page? What will 35 cents buy in personalized daily news? Today, very little—in the future, not necessarily much more.

The second economic problem with personalized daily papers is the special role of local newspaper print advertising—the stuff that actually pays for most of the daily paper. A great deal of such advertising comes from local merchants, telling consumers who they are, what they are doing right now, what is on sale this week, and why readers would want to visit them. Take away the newspaper audience, and many of these businesses disappear—and the local consumer's knowledge of when and where to shop diminishes. This is not a good thing for local economies or the local sense of community.

Then there is the social aspect of *Me* reading. Part of what the reader gets from a newspaper comes from all the headlines glanced at and from the stories that are read as a consequence, even though they would never show up in an individual's interest profile. This is one of the big advantages of the daily local paper over TV news—it has many times as much room for words and can therefore cover many more items, large and small. A typical metropolitan newspaper probably has some two hundred stories on an average day. While most readers will only read ten or twenty stories from beginning to end, all readers are aware of the other headlines, thus keeping in touch with the complexities of the real world. Some of those complexities may certainly be unpleasant. That is an attribute of nonvirtual reality. Being aware of what is happening in the wider world is critical to being part of a community and of society as a whole. The personal newspaper will not provide that connectivity.

The latter may be one reason that some people who are into virtual reality are so enamored of *The Daily Me*. How many people would have Bosnia in their personal profiles? Virtual reality is what you want it to be—it is purged of all those nasty real-world aspects. How does a person know what is of interest until he or she reads about it? Does anyone really want a daily newspaper that deals only with predetermined interests? Should we not want to broaden our horizons? Is it really the fate of humanity to become more and more narrow, more and more specialized, until we each know everything there is to know about nothing at all?

The Daily Me is inherently solipsistic: the reader becomes less and less aware of the realities of life and increasingly comfortable with only that which reinforces his or her own opinions and worldview. Currently, the primary application of personalized "newspapers" is for business alerts, at business prices. That is appropriate—but a far cry from a replacement for daily newspapers.

The daily newspaper is a wonderful institution, both as part of the economic life of a city and as a factor in socialization. It deserves to live—and, interestingly, even some Death-of-Print advocates see printed daily newspapers as long-term survivors.

Points to Remember

📖 Print is neither dying nor ailing. Books, magazines, and newspapers represent large and growing industries in the United States and abroad.

📖 More than two-thirds of all U.S. households buy books in a typical year, and more than two-thirds of adults also use public libraries. Library circulation and book sales are both increasing.

📖 The death of print and public libraries has been suggested several times in the past, when motion pictures, radio, and television became popular. Then as now, new media built their own markets—enhancements, not replacements.

📖 Print on paper is a highly refined technology, developed over several hundred years and made more cost-effective and timely by contemporary technology.

📖 People prefer the printed page to the screen for all but the shortest text passages, for sound ergonomic reasons that will not be eliminated in the near future.

📖 Linear text works exceptionally well for building understanding and enlightenment and for story telling. Most nonreference books would not benefit from hypertext.

📖 Publishers are not just printers and distributors. They also filter, refine, encourage, and publicize books and articles.

📖 Digital publishing and distribution should offer cost savings for some reference works and short-run journals and monographs, but will not offer savings for more typical books, magazines, and newspapers. Physical production and distribution costs represent a small fraction of the price of a typical book.

📖 Personalized daily "newspapers," while useful in some supplementary business applications, are impractical and undesirable replacements for today's daily newspapers. They would cost more, do less, and encourage narrow interests at the expense of societal and social awareness.

3

The Madness of Technolust

The only difference between the men and the boys is the price of their toys.

He who dies with the most toys wins.

Two popular bumper stickers of the 1980s

echnolust is widespread in many fields—including librarianship. Men appear to be more prone to the malady than women, but women are not immune. At its root, technolust is characterized by an excessive fascination with the newest toys and an unreasoning faith in the new.

It is desirable for librarians and others to be interested in, and keep up with, developments in technology and information. It is highly undesirable to succumb to technolust. People with technolust see possibilities and assume certainties. In the 1950s, it was confidently predicted that everyone would be walking around with the Library of Congress in a briefcase—courtesy of the miracle of microfiche. People with technolust look at growth rates in the first year of a new technology and project the those rates into the indefinite future. This is the technological equivalent of predicting that by 2050 *everyone* in America will be a lawyer based on the growth of the legal profession in recent decades. It has given us such absurdities as predictions of a multi-*trillion*-dollar market for multimedia

36

and personal electronics by the end of the 1990s and projected annual PC sales in excess of the size of the population.

Symptoms of Technolust

Technolust assumes that the new is always better than the old and that what is in development must be better than what just hit the market. Technojunkies snapped up thousands of Apple Newtons when that device was first introduced. No matter that the handwriting recognition technology performed so poorly that *Doonesbury* had a field day with it; no matter that the accessories that would make it a *useful* overpriced yuppie toy were not even available yet.[1] The kind phrase for such people is "early adopters." Realistically, they need a technological Twelve-Step program.

Technojunkies look at new devices and see wonderful toys or wonderful "solutions," and never seem to pause to investigate the existence of the "problem" these devices are meant to solve. Some technojunkies say that technology is a lifestyle—whatever that might mean—and proclaim books and libraries to be obsolete.

The victims of technolust (for they are victims and deserve our deep compassion) assume that every technological improvement is worthwhile and that each improvement automatically means the replacement of existing systems. When Pentium-based personal computers first came on the market, they were more than twice as expensive as equivalent 486/66 systems and showed, at best, a 20 percent improvement in performance. One has to be in the grip of a powerful compulsion to regard an expenditure of more than 200 percent for a 20 percent improvement as a bargain. Nevertheless, the technojunkie magazine reviewers said "gotta have it *now*." Sensible users waited the nine months or so that it took for the 20 percent improvement in performance to cost less than a 20 percent price hike.

---

1.   Apple appears to be repositioning the Newton as a device for various specialized purposes, a "vertical market" device, in which role it may succeed quite nicely.

Experienced users and managers know that it takes a doubling of performance to make a significant difference. For practical tool-users, Pentium PCs meant nothing for the moment. However, they *were* faster and, to a technojunkie, that was all mattered. Then the vicious spiral of technolust occurred—true technojunkies had to buy their Pentium PCs in 1993 or early 1994 because after that, PowerPCs would be out and it would be too late. Only the newest will do.

There must be people who think it is a stunning achievement to be able to watch The Beatles' *Hard Day's Night* in a small corner of a computer screen, from a CD-ROM that costs twice as much as a videocassette, even though the VCR gives several times the resolution and twenty times the size on the TV screen. Those people are either *serious* film students or technojunkies.

Technojunkies and those whom they impress will probably take our strictures as a rejection of technology. Let us repeat: anyone whose working life is affected by technology—including almost everyone in the library field—should have an active interest in new and emerging technologies. It is not only healthy but probably essential to progress and survival. An interest in the new should not be confused with neophilia, however, and it is the excessive nature of technolust that is the problem.

We could simply advise technojunkies to get a life, but there is always the danger that their technolust may impress and influence others—especially when their irresponsible fantasies promise vast savings in some indeterminate future, meanwhile increasing costs to taxpayers in the present. Technojunkies are free to spend their own resources—but any urging that libraries or other institutions should support their habits at the expense of the disadvantaged and the broader society should be resisted.

Male Fantasies and Virtual Reality?

Ed Valauskas recently commented on the concept of virtual libraries.[2] He gave information from studies by Cornelia Brun-

---

2.   Edward J. Valauskas, "Letter from the frontier," *Apple Library Users Group Newsletter*, April 1992, pp. 42–44.

ner that show differences in the way men and women view technology. Oversimplifying, men tend to want to recreate the universe through technology—in other words, technojunkies see technology as an end in itself. On the other hand, technologically-knowledgeable members of the Sensible Gender want to use technology to connect people. That is the tool-user's approach—seeing technology as significant only when it is a means to desired ends.

To quote Valauskas: "what better way to 'correct' our [librarians'] social image than by trashing entirely the notion of books in paper, reading words sequentially, using indices to locate ideas. Instead, *hyperanthropos*, Lucian's HyperMan, running the operation at his mighty computer keyboard." Valauskas' own conclusion:

> Give me real books . . . for the time being, and a real library. I may have CD-ROMs, electronic journals, microfilm, microfiche, books and periodicals on diskette, software, cassettes, computers, and videos in my library, but paper still seems to be a quite popular medium. And the statistics back me up . . . Let's just hope that we use technology not as a means to re-invent libraries in a ridiculous self-image, but as a vehicle to reach a broader audience even better than we do right now.[3]

Technolust—Some Case Studies

Victims of technolust assume that each new device will succeed, and succeed brilliantly. One feature of the syndrome is selective amnesia, enabling the technojunkie to greet each false dawn with high hopes. Market analysts of the technolust persuasion assured us two years ago that by now tens of millions of Americans would have CD-I or CD-V or VIS or some other CD-based system attached to our TV sets—and they still talk of the about-to-explode home computing market, and claim there will be 2.2 computers in every household by 1999.[4] These are

---

3. Ibid.

4. Channel Marketing Corporation, Dallas, as reported by *Newsbytes*, March 3, 1992.

the same prophets who assume a "digital convergence" in which all analog media will become part of the great digital highway—not because of any evidence that people wish to give up books, magazines, videocassettes, and the like or that their lives would be better if they did, but simply because the digital highway is possible.

Of course, in the virtual reality of the futurists (as opposed to the real world of achievable technology and market forces), the masses of people using CD-I or CD-V or VIS use them with wall-mounted flat-screen TVs. Technojunkies of a decade ago assured us that cathode ray tubes (CRTs) would be long gone by now—and continue to assure us that CRTs are on the way out, even though in 1994 an 11-inch VGA color liquid crystal display (LCD) screen costs $6,000, and it appears to be impossible to buy a 14-inch SuperVGA LCD screen. Meanwhile, a top-of-the-line 17-inch CRT-based display cost around $1,000 in late 1994. The CRT is an established (even old) technology—but it keeps getting better. Only someone with a terminal case of technolust would trade in a 17-inch CRT, or even a 15-inch CRT, for a much more expensive 11-inch LCD screen.

The One-Centimeter Rolls

There is a chestnut about the pace of technological change in the computer field. It goes something like this: if cars had developed on the same curve as computers, a Rolls-Royce would now cost $2.50 and get 1,000 miles to the gallon. The kicker is that the Rolls Royce would be one centimeter long. It is human to indulge in hyperbole and oversimplification at times. It is foolishness to do it all the time.

It is essential that those of us involved and interested in communication technology step back, view developments rationally, and place trends in broader perspectives. Technojunkies look at each new device and project all of its possibilities while being sublimely indifferent to even obvious drawbacks. In the grip of technolust, it seems quite logical to take a three-year growth pattern and extend it for a decade. In the real world, such projections make no sense whatsoever.

Technojunkies make no distinction between *obsolescent*—the state of most real-world devices—and *obsolete*—a different thing altogether. *Anything* that has reached the market is on its way to obsolescence. In the long or short term, everything is replaced by something newer. Human beings are, from one point of view, obsolescent—it is just that we are not sure yet what will replace us. Any new PC is obsolescent—it is, after all, available for sale, always a sure sign. *Obsolete* is something very different: an obsolete item is no longer useful and has been wholly superseded. As one dictionary puts it, "No longer active or in use . . . formerly but no longer current."[5] New devices do not automatically make old devices obsolete; for one thing they may lack some capabilities of the older technology.

Wired People

A special kind of technolust is found in the technojunkies of the Internet—the preference for virtual reality over, how shall we put it? . . . reality. These are people who would really rather read text on a screen than on a page, simply because it *is* on the screen. Wired People assume that a periodic table available over the Internet must be right—after all, it is on the Net—even if some of the symbols are wrong and it seems to be missing a couple of dozen elements. Wired People send out questions and assume that the answers they get must be correct—they have been sanctified by the Net—but really have no time to deal with the answers because they are too busy with something new on the Net.

This strain of technolust is most difficult to deal with. It blinds its victims to reality in general. Because their access to, and use of, the Internet is subsidized by a university, they assume that the Internet is free and assert, therefore, that all information *should* be free, or at least free to them. Does it cost anything to generate and organize information? Maybe, but that is not their problem. So it goes, and the Wired People manage to maintain a willful denial of the possibility that, in a so-called information society, some people might expect to earn a living dealing with information. Of course, many of the Wired People earn their living by processing information—quite a different kettle of fish.

---

5. *Oxford English dictionary*, 2nd ed., Oxford: Clarendon Press, 1989.

Technolust in Libraries

John Buschmann has raised some compelling points about technolust in libraries.[6] He suggests that electronic resources are perceived as having a higher status than print resources, and that science materials are perceived as having a higher status than those in the social science and humanities. This suggestion explains a lot about budgetary decisions in some academic libraries and may help to explain the number of seemingly thoughtful and experienced library leaders who have succumbed to a simplistic all-digital view of the future.

Why Technolust Matters

Technolust is a malady that causes depression. A person who truly believes that newer is always better is doomed to perpetual disappointment—whatever is bought is inadequate because there is always something newer and better just around the corner. As for those who believe that the Net is all that matters . . . well, they are probably not reading this anyway. Unfortunately, we cannot just heave a sigh for the victims of technolust and move on. Technolust matters and must be combated because of its effects on rational discourse and reasonable planning for the future. It matters in at least five separate ways:

♦ Technolust victims make extreme forecasts concerning the future of new technologies and the death of existing technologies. Those projections sometimes carry more weight than they should (some technolust victims seem like reasonable people), and make rational planning more difficult as a result.

♦ Technojunkies do not listen to differing viewpoints. They know what is right, and dismiss other viewpoints as being old-fashioned and retrograde.

---

6. John Buschmann, "Librarians, self-censorship, and information technologies," *College & Research Libraries*, May 1994, pp. 221–228.

◆ Technojunkies do not understand real-world economics very well. Since many of them live in subsidized ivory towers compounded by virtual reality, that is scarcely surprising. Because some aspects of computing have become more cost effective by orders of magnitude in the past few years, technojunkies often assume that all technology is, or soon will be, so cheap that cost ceases to be a factor. Thus, the solution to the cost barrier to any wonderful technological innovation is simply a matter of time. This leads to a mind-set in which issues such as intellectual property rights, salaries, etc., are simply not worth discussing.

◆ Technolust assumes and asserts a simple future, one in which technology solves all problems and new technologies always replace older ones with a minimum of fuss and dislocation. This sanitized view of the world resembles nothing so much as an intellectual theme park. We will march forward into this new and wonderful virtual world, in which we will all have wonderful jobs made possible by the wonders of ever-improving technology.

◆ Technojunkies are very good at keeping up with new technology. They're not so good at making such technology a smoothly functioning part of the workplace, or at dealing with the everyday issues involved in introducing new technology. After all, by the time the stuff has actually arrived, it is already old hat—real technojunkies want something newer and better.

New Technologies and Old

There is an unnerving fact that needs to be remembered whenever one considers marvelous new devices and trends. *Most innovations fail!* Sometimes they fail before reaching the market; sometimes very shortly afterwards; sometimes after a brief blaze of glory; and sometimes after apparently becoming established in solid markets.

Libraries have been caught by failures in media (mass-market and specialized) in the past. They would be well advised not to be caught by electronic innovations as well. Remember eight-track tapes, an apparent success that failed completely? Remember Beta—or, more significantly, the half-dozen videocassette systems introduced *before* Sony marketed Beta? Some libraries must have established Cartrivision or SelectaVision or V-Cord collections, and many libraries still use U-Matic tapes— all monuments to a future that never was.

How about videodiscs? At least half a dozen systems were attempted (the earliest in 1928), and the trail of failures pretty much ends in 1984, when RCA abandoned its dismal CED system. RCA managed to derail marketing efforts for LaserVision, keeping it from establishing an early large market share— but Pioneer stuck with it, and there is some reason to believe that LaserVision, already a success in industrial markets, will be a long-term consumer success.

Information Technology Devices

The record of innovation in information technology is no better than elsewhere. Remember ultrafiche and micro-opaques? How about Cauzin Data Strips, a technology so promising that *PC World* was publishing software using the strips for a couple of years? How about digital paper? That was promoted as the hot new thing about a decade ago—and, every year since, we have heard that it will revolutionize storage as soon as it really hits the market—if it ever does. Today there is holographic storage. "Not quite ready for market yet, old boy, but it will replace everything when it is." Another inevitable smash hit.

Then there is CD-ROM—well known to be an "instantaneous success." The standards for CD-ROMs were established in 1983. The first products, for libraries, came out in 1984. Predictions of instant mass-market success began in 1987; seven years later, those predictions are still being made and confounded. By late 1994, millions of personal computers had CD-ROM drives, but best-selling nongame CD-ROMs were still few and far between. Meanwhile, libraries may still be the largest market for CD-ROM-based information (as opposed to software, clip art, and typefaces) and informed librarians understand that

CD-ROMs are useful tools despite being a relatively low technology by today's standards.

The Dismal Fate of "Sure-Fire Successes"

How could anyone have predicted that CD-ROM, from the Eurocentric company Philips with its erratic U.S. marketing, would be *the* successful optical medium? Around the same time that CD-ROMs came out, 3M announced OROM (to be developed in partnership with IBM). In 1988, OROM appeared to be the coming thing. So, in the mid-1980s, did Sony's DataROM. OROM seems to have disappeared without a trace other than as the niche-market 128MB optical disk. DataROM may have mutated into Sony's MiniDisc, a recordable audio medium.

The MiniDisc has potential as a data storage medium—but with only 128-megabyte storage capacity as compared to the 600MB of CD-ROM.[7] Drexel's LaserCard has been around for four or five years. It, at least, has succeeded in certain niche markets but has made no impact on the mass market.

There are a plethora of "sure things" on the market now. Only one or two will meet with real success. In the individual consumer market, there are four or five different, incompatible disc-video technologies: VIS, CD-Video, CD-Interactive, and others. Some have already failed; some are still heralded as the next big thing. In the world of microcomputers, there are such innovations as the 2.88MB diskette drive, the 21MB floptical drive, several incompatible removable mass-storage devices . . . and the beat goes on.

Survival: Not Always Predictable

We have already noted that the cathode ray tube (CRT) was supposed to be long gone by now and that its imminent replacement has been a staple prediction for some two decades now.

---

7.   MiniDisc achieves its 75-minute audio capacity by throwing away most of the recorded information, based on computer models of what a person can actually hear at any moment. This may be an elegant *audio* solution but clearly cannot apply to texts: it is impossible to discard 75 percent of a text based on what can be read at any moment!

CRTs are archaic in terms of general technological development, but they keep getting better—thus making a moving target for replacement technologies. If anything, the gap between CRTs and thin-screen devices seems to be growing.

Speaking of dead ducks, consider hard disks. Several well-considered projections half a decade back showed solid-state memory, with its far superior speed and resistance to crashing, becoming cheaper than hard disks within five years. That has come true—random access memory (RAM) is now cheaper than hard disk storage was five years ago, and even the kind of stable RAM needed for solid-state disks is about where hard disks were five or six years ago. The catch is, of course, that hard disks are considerably cheaper and faster now than they were then. An attentive listener can almost hear the engineers who have brought down the price of durable RAM—"Well, we made it for $100 a megabyte; what more do you want?" Alas for them, the answer is that hard disk storage costs about $0.60 to $1.00 a megabyte. The target has moved and the job has become tougher. To top it off, today's hard disk drives are at least ten times as durable as those of a few years ago. It is now quite rare for a contemporary disk drive to suffer a mechanical crash.

The Library as Museum of Failed Technology

Why dwell on these failures? (Please note we have only mentioned a few examples of many.) The answer is librarians have been urged to use almost every one of these innovations immediately to protect their libraries from becoming irrelevant—and some libraries have done so. What is the library to do after the new technology is shown to be a failure? Easy—transfer the resources to a current digital medium such as write-once optical disks or digital audio tape (which has gone from "next big thing" to niche-market product in a matter of months). Easy, but who has the money or time to do that?

In practice, one of two things happens: either the resources (some of which may be unique) are rendered inaccessible or the library becomes, as many have, a museum of failed technology. In the latter case there is the ever-growing expense and drain on the spirit of having to maintain the unviable so that the resources are available. Librarianship will continue to need some such museums, but should take urgent steps to prevent their numbers from growing.

That is particularly true because newer media require players that are more difficult to maintain those of the older media. Any skilled craftsperson with the proper lenses could build a new ultrafiche reader; will that be true of CD-ROM if it ever becomes obsolete? Even now, one has to wonder how many historically important wire recordings sit in archives, museums, and libraries that no longer have working wire recorders. Few libraries can afford to be in the vanguard of each innovation. When is the time right? There is no easy answer, but erring on the side of caution is likely to serve libraries better than rushing to adopt untested technologies.

The New Is Not Always Better

The United Kingdom has suffered for decades because it was the first country to have an industrial revolution. The new is not always better and the later life of a pioneer is likely to be unhappy. Some old ways continue to make perfectly good sense and some innovations are the more rewarding after someone else has tested them. Quite often, new things are neither successful nor correct, as those who have bought the first version of a new computer or the first release of new software know only too well. To take some examples;

- ◆ Is video from a CD-ROM or via the Internet better than video from a laserdisc? Certainly not for viewing—its quality is lower and it is far more resource intensive. Those who need to manipulate the image *and* have the right to do so might prefer the newer method but for most the laserdisc is better.

- ◆ Is an LCD screen better than a CRT? All else being equal it may be. However, all else will not be equal until a 15-inch 800-by-600 LCD able to display at least 64,000 simultaneous colors costs less than $500—or, rather, what a comparable CRT costs at that point. For now, it makes sense to stick with the 60-year-old CRT technology.

♦ Is a Sony Data Discman better than a printed paperback? It could be for a few quick reference texts, but it certainly is not when it comes to pleasure reading on an airplane, at the beach, over breakfast. The idea of reading a whole book or any major fraction of it on the best PowerBook or notebook computer is appalling, and it is likely that few people have ever done it. The Data Discman seems much worse, and it seems unlikely that Sony regards the Data Discman as a replacement for books in general.[8]

Should we turn in our 486/66 systems and laser printers for manual typewriters? Absolutely not. There are many cases in which the new is indeed better. It makes sense to follow new technology and to look for effective ways to use new technology—but only when that technology is appropriate, when it offers a clear advantage, and when the technology is likely to succeed. Each innovation should be viewed with an informed, skeptical eye blinded neither by glitter nor by nostalgia.

New and Older Technologies

Change, Not Displacement

With relatively few exceptions, new technologies complement and change older ones. When they do displace them, they do so over time and to the extent that the new technologies offer demonstrable advantages. This is particularly true of the technology of communication. Print did not destroy the oral tradition—it extended its reach. Cinema did not destroy live theater. Radio news did not destroy newspapers. Even television, which has apparently hurt newspaper circulation to some extent, has changed rather than obliterated newspapers. Television did not destroy radio, which is more popular now than ever, although it did change radio's direction.

Television and home video have had a profound effect on the motion picture business—but in complex ways still not

---

8.   Olaf Olafsson, president of Sony Electronic Publishing, has commented "I just don't personally believe in reading novels on a computer screen." Quoted in D. T. Max, "The end of the book?" *Atlantic Monthly*, September 1994, pp. 61–71.

fully understood, and ways that have certainly not destroyed the motion picture industry. Widespread, inexpensive electronic distribution, either in physical form such as CD-ROM or in virtual form such as the Internet, will not destroy books, newspapers and magazines—although, again, the uses and structures of print will surely change. We see here a perfect paradigm of technological change—one in which the "weak" uses of print-on-paper will either disappear or diminish greatly, while the "strong" forms will survive and thrive.

It is safe to assume that electronic distribution and digital publishing will make their marks as new media—just as each new medium has done in the past. Some of this can be seen already. *From Alice to Ocean* is a book and CD-ROM package. The CD-ROM publisher who acquired rights to Randy Shilts' *Conduct Unbecoming* will release the text on CD-ROM, with full-text search capabilities. However, the major point of the CD-ROM will be video interviews with some of the people in the book—and the publisher regards the CD-ROM as a complement to the printed book, not an alternative. The revealing diaries of the late H. R. Haldeman have been published in book form and on CD-ROM with accompanying newsreels and other video resources—the book is a mass-market bestseller and the CD-ROM a paradise for Watergate buffs. Only the most fervid futurists and some fellow-traveling librarians still speak of electronic "books" as imminent and inevitable replacements for printed books. Let us not forget that some librarians asserted that print and libraries were doomed when TV came along, when radio came along, even when sound recording came along. History has nothing to teach those with simplistic views.

When considering the future of print, it is essential to remember that, within a broad technology, the new improves and sustains the old. That is as true of print publishing as of any other technology—maybe even more so. Twenty years ago, it took a very expensive Linotype or Monotype machine and a skilled operator to set type for a book. This posed a major entry barrier to new publishers because it imposed a substantial cost to put ink on paper. Today, anyone with a $1,500 computer and $600 printer can produce camera-ready pages with more typographic flexibility than the old systems, at a per-page cost of 2.5 cents. Compare the latter to the $6 to $10 a page of a Linotype process. Improvements in short-run printing and binding lower other entry barriers to startup publishers. Even as conglomerates reduce the number of old established, independent publishing houses, there has been a technological revolution that has enabled the establishment of new companies producing fully competitive books.

The exciting thing is that revolution is by no means over. Today, we are to the point at which short-run full-color printing can be done economically and rapidly, by systems that go directly from the PC to the press with no intervening steps. Within a few years, a library may be able to publish its own full-color art book using a local contract printer, in a run of 1,000 copies for production costs of $5 to $10 per copy. The computer has been seen as the enemy of the book by futurists and book people alike. The reverse is the truth. Each has a secure place in any feasible future and each will strengthen the other.

The Exception That Proves the Rule?

Futurists often mention audio CDs as a case showing that new technology can totally displace an older one quite rapidly and move from there to predict the death of print-on-paper. The audio CD is an exceptional case; moreover, the premise of the argument is somewhat shaky. Vinyl discs were already being displaced by audiocassettes—they were a minority sound medium before CDs came along. More to the point, vinyl discs represented fundamentally flawed technology. Each use of a vinyl disc tends to destroy it and vinyl discs need exceptional care to work well in the first place. People moved to audiocassettes not because they were higher quality (they are of significantly lower quality) but because cassettes are much more convenient: they are portable, they do not require agonies of cleaning, anti-static treatment, etc., and their sound quality does not deteriorate as rapidly or dramatically as vinyl discs. CDs combine almost the same convenience as cassettes with sound quality as good as or better than that of vinyl discs; they sound as good on the twentieth playing as on the first; and the consumer does not need to be a tweak to set CD equipment up properly.

Books, magazines and newspapers would be ripe for the trashing if they were as inconvenient as vinyl discs *and* if there were inexpensive, acceptable alternatives. They are not inconvenient and there is no foreseeable alternative—the CD analogy is inapt.

Ideology and the Marketplace

Given the clear history of communication technology and the established facts of the marketplace, why do projections of the death of print continue? Not because of present and likely future reality. Instead, such projections tend to be based on ideology and projection. The ideology is the belief that electronic information is somehow superior. The projection lies in the attitude that an individual's wants and needs are shared by everyone else. Anyone who reads computer columnists is familiar with projection. Because computer journalists think they need to be in touch with everyone else 24 hours a day and have notebook computers with them at all times, they see such things as necessities of life. These are people who tend to have local area networks at home—scarcely a plausible basis for projecting other people's needs!

The specific ideologies pushed by the futurists are slippery and hard to define, but they all tend to sweep aside matters of copyright; intellectual property; authenticity; the value of linear text; and the difference between data, information, knowledge, understanding, and wisdom. These people see that some reference works can be more current and usable in electronic form—as librarians know—and conclude that all printed materials fall into the category of reference works. After all, all that counts is having more and newer information, right?

Synecdoche Can Be Dangerous to Your Mental Health

Another problem leading some librarians to extreme projections is synecdoche—taking the part for the whole. A distinguished librarian reads a report from one scientific organization suggesting that most communications within that particular field will be electronic in another 20 years. The librarian jumps from that report to the assertion that *all* scholarly communication will be electronic in another 20 years, and from there to the assumption that collections of print material will no longer be relevant. Yet another librarian, reading this assertion that relates to university libraries, adds to the confusion by assuming that all libraries will be electronic (if they exist at all) and in a few years, not in 20 years.

The practices of one scholarly field are not those of all fields. There is no reason to assume, for example, that historians and philosophers will suddenly become as enamored of electronic communication as physicists. Moreover, the practices of the future do not negate the past and present: even if most future articles in physics are prepared and distributed electronically, the foundations for those future articles will be in print. The lesson is clear: rational analysis and clear thinking will enable all of us to cope with the complex, multi-medium library of the future using technology with intelligence.

Points to Remember

📖 The new complements the old, even when the old is changed.

📖 Most new devices fail. Technological success is rarely predictable.

📖 New techniques revive and sustain old technologies. That explains the continued success of CRTs and hard disks—it is also why startup print publishers can produce fully competitive books far faster and less expensively than a decade ago.

📖 Most people adopt new devices because they fulfill a need, real or perceived; devices are tools for scratching itches. Most people are not swayed by ideology—if the itch is not widely felt or if marketers cannot communicate that this is the best way to scratch it, the quality of the device is immaterial.

4

Electronic Publishing and Distribution

The question of the future of publishing has become a battleground of warring extremists. On our left we have the person who, seeing that it makes sense to replace the print *Books in Print* with a more current, more easily accessible electronic version, concludes that the same is true of Kant's *Critique of Pure Reason*. On our right we have the person who sees something sacred in the very existence of print-on-paper and insists that the local *Yellow Pages* is an artifact of inherent value. These absurd positions are based on faith not rationality and we can only stand and watch as the yahoo who hates books runs full tilt into the bookist who hates all media of communication *but* books.

In considering electronic publishing, we need to understand its economics and its limitations and strengths. Libraries must not be hostile to electronic publishing, but neither should they expect it to be a simple answer to the ever-escalating costs of acquiring and storing books and other non-electronic documents. There will be an increase in electronic publishing—the scale and timing of that increase are much more problematic.

We can learn about the future relationship between libraries and electronic publishing by looking at our recent past. Libraries were the first important market for CD-ROM as a medium of publication and are one of the most important markets to this day. Libraries have also been among the chief customers of online searching services—an established form of electronic dissemination. Libraries will remain major and effective users of electronic publications of all kinds and this use will forge a complex and central relationship between future libraries and electronic publishers and distributors.

Not every form of electronic publication makes economic and practical sense. It is edifying to look at sensible applications of electronic publishing and at some of the failures in this area.

Some Print Publications That Should Disappear

We spend a lot of money purchasing, storing, and making accessible print publications that would be cheaper, more current, and easier to use if they were available to libraries in electronic form via CD-ROM, imaging systems, or online. Here are some of them.

♦ Any print-on-paper product that is used primarily on a paragraph-by-paragraph (or smaller unit) basis and in which the currency of information is vital to its effectiveness. Such documents include ready reference works (dictionaries, indexes, gazetteers, almanacs, etc.) and statistical compilations.

♦ Any collective print product, serial or monographic, for which the probable use is less than one-tenth of the whole over the life of the edition. The most obvious example is that of back runs of little-used serials, especially if the articles in them can be transferred to a sophisticated search and retrieval system. Other possibilities are runs of government documents and conference proceedings.

♦ Any print-on-paper product for which the delays caused by print production and distribution are such that the data or organized information in it is outdated by the time the publication is available. Consumer and price guides and financial information of all kinds come readily to mind. However, libraries and publishers must weigh the cost and benefit of transferring the means of communication, and it is our belief that when cost-benefit is assessed objectively, the number of publications that fall into this category is smaller than some futurists would have us believe.

Some Electronic Publishing Schemes That Do Not Work

Most librarians are aware of sensible and successful forays into electronic publishing and look forward to sensible proposals coming to fruition in the future. Unfortunately, the history of electronic publishing thus far is also replete with examples that range from the noble failure to the hare-brained. Let us look at some instances of CD-ROM publications and online text systems that teach us what to avoid in the future.

CD-ROM Publications for the Home?

The "Library-of-the-Month Club"

The science fiction writer and computer columnist Jerry Pournelle has, in the past, floated the idea of the "Library-of-the-Month Club"—subscription CD-ROMs with 500 to 1,000 book-length texts on each monthly disc.[1] Predicated on the anticipated universal availability of CD-ROM readers in the home, the rest flows naturally. Charge, say, about $20 per month (affordable if based on a wild guess), sell millions of the discs: the subscribers are happy and the entrepreneurs are happy. Seems unbeatable, but there are one or two flaws.

In practice, readers' tastes vary so much that hundreds of such clubs would be needed—and few readers manage more than one or two books a week. Thus, a typical reader with

---

1.   Pournelle hinted at this concept in various columns in *Byte Magazine*, *InfoWorld*, and elsewhere during the late 1980s and early 1990s, including comments in the March 1985, April 1986, and June 1988 issues of *Byte Magazine*. This discussion extrapolates from various notes over that time.

focused interests would be receiving at least 50 times as many books as he or she could read; a reader with diverse interests, several hundred times as many.

More significantly, such libraries-of-the-month, realistically reaching much smaller audiences, could not be so inexpensive. Most writers in the real world expect some royalties for their efforts; even for original paperbacks, such royalties will be at least 30 to 50 cents per copy. Thus, royalties for a 500-book CD-ROM would be at least $150 to $250 per copy. Given the realities of marketing, distribution, publisher overhead and profit, the subscription price of a library-of-the-month would be at least $250 to $400 *per month*: the price of anywhere from 10 hardbound to 50 or 60 paperback originals. Such a product, requiring a commitment of $3,000 to $4,800 per year to receive more "books" than could possibly be read, seems unlikely to set the world on fire.

Magazines on CD-ROM

One futurist has stated that collections of magazines delivered to the home on CD-ROM should replace printed magazines any day now. This assertion is based on the fact that one can purchase a Sony Data Discman for under $600. "More magazines than you could possibly want" would be delivered on a CD-ROM each month and they could be read on the screen of the Discman or, if it were attached to a home computer, copies of articles could be printed, cited, etc. "The utility has improved tremendously and the cost is minimal at best."[2]

This scenario does not stand up to even the most cursory analysis. It would work *if*

♦ there were any evidence that the high production values of inexpensive printed magazines could even be approximated by such a system;

♦ there were any evidence of a public willing to sacrifice the convenience and low cost of those magazines for the ability to cut and paste, print selectively, etc.;

2.   Sanjay R. Chadha, "Virtual libraries continued," electronic message distributed over PACS-L listserv, February 21, 1992.

♦ the small monochrome screen of the Discman were an acceptable substitute for the readability and appeal of the high quality text and sophisticated full color graphics of modern printed magazines;

♦ everyone wanted the same magazines so there would not have to be a separate CD-ROM pressing for each one; and

♦ advertisers (who carry the cost of mass market printed magazines) could be persuaded to switch to the new medium in which, after all, their advertisements would not normally be the items selected for printing, cutting and pasting, etc.

Full-text magazine collections on CD-ROM may have a place in libraries, even though they are not true substitutes for printed issues. They appear, however, to have no future for home use.

The Dream of the CD-ROM Mass Market

The library-of-the-month club and the death of the printed magazine are just two of the dreams that make up the larger dream of the mass market CD-ROM. There have been many other manifestations of the dream and all have run full tilt into the central question: *just what is it that people want to buy in 600-megabyte quantities*? Moreover, what is it that they want so badly that they will set up a computer system to run it?

CD-ROM drives are becoming popular for powerful new personal computers, including those purchased for use at home. There are several reasons for this, not the least of which is that CD-ROM is a wonderful distribution medium for large computer programs, collections of clip art, and collections of typefaces. Sales figures of the CD-ROMs themselves are quite another story. Most surveys show that 90 percent of all the CD-ROMs ever bought for a drive are bought within the first 45 days after the drive itself is purchased, and we suspect that many of these purchases are really a hidden part of the cost of the drive purchase.

Is there a true mass market for CD-ROMs as publications? It is hard to see that there is one or that there will be one in the foreseeable future. "Best-selling" CD-ROM encyclopedias have gone down substantially in price and there does seem to be a niche for sales at the very low end of the price range—*but* remember, only a minuscule number of best-selling CD-ROMs can be considered *publications*. What people *will* buy on CD-ROM, apparently, is fancier and fancier games. It should be apparent to even the most starry-eyed by now that game systems do not represent the foot in the door that opens for later, more substantial information use. Game systems are openings for more game systems and nothing else outside the home entertainment field.

Let us look at the CD-ROM publications that are available now. "Electronic books" is an interesting term used by those who foresee the supplanting of real books by electronic communications. It is relevant to note that the word "book" is still seen as a selling point in the mass market. These CD-ROM texts sell for between $19 and $50; much higher than the price range of paperbacks, which do not require a prior expenditure on equipment. Collections of paintings and other art works seem to be a natural for CD-ROMs—until the realization dawns that the picture quality is greatly inferior to that of a decent art book.

Perhaps the best possibility is that suggested by Michael Schrage,[3] who suggests that some books should be sold with a CD-ROM version in a pocket in the back cover. That combination provides readability in the book version combined with the fast searching and specialized access possible on CD-ROM. The combination has already happened with the *Random House Unabridged Dictionary*, but in few other cases. Even if this practice were to become common, it certainly would not portend the death of print.

The newest hype is for "multimedia"—CD-ROM based systems that incorporate text, sounds, and images. Of course, in order to exploit these publications, purchasers will need to upgrade their PCs or Macintoshes by adding suitable sound equipment, having a fast enough CD-ROM player to make it work, and so on. The result will be that one can incorporate moving pictures and stereo sound. One is then able to spend $60 on a Beethoven symphony that also provides lots of things

---

3.   Michael Schrage, "The next page in book publishing history should be a digitized one," *Los Angeles Times*, September 2, 1993.

to look at on the screen while the music is playing. If the purchaser is studying music, such an expenditure might make sense. For the average classical music lover, $60 will buy two or three full-priced symphonies on audio compact disc with quite a bit left over for a good book on Beethoven and his music.

Another thing for the would-be multimedia purchaser to check out is the video component. Compare the video in multimedia systems to ordinary VHS cassettes. The former is greatly inferior. If this is an unfair comparison, ask why the purchaser should spend so much more for a CD-ROM than for a cheap videocassette with superior visual quality and near-CD quality sound (an attribute of most modern videocassettes).

CD-ROM is well adapted to many large niche markets, including large software and data distribution applications and a number of interesting library applications. Even multimedia has its place, though that place will be far less extensive than its enthusiasts predict. However, CD-ROM has a long way to go before it establishes itself as a true mass market product.

Online Texts?

Project Gutenberg

Michael Hart began Project Gutenberg more than 20 years ago. The object of this exercise is to transfer hundreds of printed texts (all out of copyright, for obvious reasons) into electronic form and thus to create a universally available, comprehensive "electronic library" that will replace libraries entirely. In Hart's words, the "library" of the future will consist of:

> Computer searchable collections which can be transmitted via disks, phone lines, or other media at a fraction of the cost in money, time, and paper as with present day paper media. These electronic books will not have to be reserved and restricted to use by one patron at one time. All materials will be available to all patrons from all locations at all times.[4]

---

4. Michael Hart, "Project Gutenberg: access to electronic texts," *Database*, December 1990, pp. 6–9.

Gutenberg's role in this is to "provide a collection of 10,000 of the most-used books by the year 2000 and to reduce . . . the effective price to the user to approximately one cent per book plus the cost of media and of shipping and handling."[5] Sounds great, no? Let us leave aside, for the moment, the hundreds of thousands of texts that *are* in copyright, the practical utility of such a scheme, and the unsubstantiated "savings" in money and paper. Let us also leave aside the fact that one of the authors of this book works in a modest university library with a collection of 860,000 plus books that were used (by being borrowed and by being read in the library) more than one million times in the last year for which complete figures are available.

Hart has asserted that Project Gutenberg has already been responsible for "giving away" 24 *billion* texts. His arithmetic is as follows. Project Gutenberg has made 240 electronic texts available on the networks thus far. There will be 100 million people with access to the Internet by the year 2000. Ergo, 240 times 100,000,000 equals 24 billion.

It is truly audacious to claim that posting a text somewhere on the Internet counts as "giving it away" to anyone who has access, *or may eventually have access*, to the network. Further, there are not 100 million people on the Internet[6] and the vast majority of those people have not the slightest interest in downloading and printing copies of widely available texts that they could purchase in easy-to-read paperback editions for $4 to $6. None of this matters in the world of e-text distribution. In the anti-math of that virtual world, the minute use of Project Gutenberg texts adds up to 24 billion and growing!

Project Gutenberg and similar schemes have some utility for those academics interested in textual analysis and those wishing to cite non-copyright materials in their own writings. It is a pity that it is being sold as the force driving the creation of the global "virtual library;" the abolition of books, printed communication and storage, and physical libraries; and the

---

5.   Michael Hart, "Information about Project Gutenberg," BITNET communication, May 11, 1990. *Cited in* Reva Basch, "Books online," *Online*, July 1991, pp. 13–23.

6.   Recent estimates of active Internet users range anywhere from 2 to 20 million, with some knowledgeable observers tending toward lower estimates.

reduction of librarians to $5-a-minute "900-number" consultants to wanderers in the electronic desert. This is pure nonsense, slice it whichever way you will, and only the deep credulous will be persuaded of its value.

Project Xanadu

Theodor Holm (Ted) Nelson has been dreaming of his stately electronic pleasure dome for more than 30 years. It is to his enduring credit that he conceived "hypertext" before personal computers existed, and that concept has led to an enormously valuable, though narrowly applicable, methodology for organizing information. He has also had Project Xanadu in mind all these years—a project that would create a vast omnimedia, interactive, fee-based, hypertext system in which every single textual, numerical, visual, and auditory record of humankind would be stored and made available at the stroke of a key or the click of a mouse. Paragraphs, data, sounds, and graphics would link in endless, limitless combinations. Nelson has improved our field by his creative thinking. Project Xanadu is no dream, however; it is an incredible and diversionary nightmare.

Nelson has written extensively on Xanadu[7] and his vision of hypertext gone global—of a worldwide network containing everything that has ever been written, recorded, or pictured—is immensely alluring to the technodreamer. He or she is wreathed in smiles imagining a world in which a credit card inserted into an information kiosk is the key to an electronic paradise in which the most wonderful navigation tools are available to find anything that anyone could conceivably want and to make all the links and leaps that enhance the value of the knowledge and information sought. Authors are protected in Xanadu—not by retaining control over their intellectual property and its integrity, for that tends to disappear in the global hypertext universe—but in terms of royalties. Each time something that is marked as the creation of an individual is touched by the voyager in Xanadu, a credit is made to the author's account. Wait a minute, though! What is to stop the voyager from taking the author's work, changing it and reissuing it as his or her own?

---

7. See, for example, Theodor Nelson, "Managing immense storage," *Byte* 13 (January 1988), pp. 225–233.

Nothing at all, but there we go again, dragging dreary old copyright into the discussion and spoiling all the fun.

It is all too wonderful. Ideas will build on ideas; sounds, images and words will dance in intricate display; and connections to worlds of learning and leisure will take the Xanadu voyager in directions undreamed of. How could boring old books, records, films, etc., possibly survive in the face of such competition? *Project Xanadu is coming to town any day now!*

Alas, that has been said now for more than a decade. Not for nothing has the Xanadu Hypermedia Information Server been said to be perhaps "the most enduring piece of vaporware in the history of the computer industry."[8] The dreamers have been cheered by the fact that the Xanadu Operating Company was controlled and, more importantly, financed by Autodesk. In their view, that made Xanadu serious. It is not necessarily so. Autodesk has used some of the profits from its one big success (Autocad) to experiment with such interesting ideas as *Chaos: the Software* and Rudy Rucker's *Cellular Automata Lab*, each of which is a wonderfully interesting graphics system of questionable commercial potential. Clearly, someone at Autodesk thought that Project Xanadu was a neat idea if not a sure-fire money maker. Sadly, Autodesk announced some time ago that they were "spinning off" the Xanadu Operating Company—that is, getting rid of it. Apparently, the company finally realized the economic reality of Xanadu.

The Electronic Invisible College

For the time being, the Internet, BITNET, etc., have created a gigantic, global medium for electronic communication that is freely available and sometimes "free" to its millions of users. It may be that, in a few years, we will look back and see this as a golden age. This Early Internet period may well turn out to be to electronic communication what the 1960s were to politics and society. For a brief time, everything seems possible in this accidentally-created electronic democracy, thousands of elec-

---

8.   Reva Basch, op cit., p. 18.

tronic flowers are blooming, and the worldwide Haight-Ash-bury is no further away than the nearest terminal.

What is it that the intellectual community is doing with this unprecedented freedom? Why, carrying on the invisible college of old by other, better means. The idea of the invisible college has been around for a very long time. In 1743, a biographer of Robert Boyle quoted him: "The Invisible College refers to that assembly of learned and curious gentlemen who . . . at length gave birth to the Royal Society" and in 1962 Derek de Solla Price wrote of "prepublication duplicated sheets circulated to the new Invisible College."9

The curious gentlemen of the Royal Society exchanged their thoughts in letters and privately printed pamphlets circulated to the elect few. The harried academics of the early 1960s exchanged letters and typescripts to colleagues within and without their own university. The Internet has democratized that process. Now anyone—scholar, knave, or crank—can read and write messages of all kinds and communicate with fellow members of subsets of the invisible college on topics from philosophy to fetishism, Byzantine ecclesiology to modern Polish political humor.

The Internet is a populist, anarchistic, quirky intellectual playground in which ideas, data, insults, comments, drafts, comments on drafts, and on and on are exchanged at a rate that defies rational use. It is *not* a substitute for the relatively ordered, filtered world of print publishing and it is *not* (as surprisingly many educated people assume it to be) free!

There is talk of charging for use of the Internet, of systems that will meter that use and restrict access to the network, of shifting the burden of payment for the network from institutions and the government to the individuals who use it. What will happen to the Internet invisible college if that comes to pass? No one knows, but it is safe to predict that both the diversity and the craziness will lessen and that the iron heel of economics will transform the Internet into something more restricted in terms of content and access. For the moment, though, the Internet invisible college has revived an almost lost form of communication: the broadside.

---

9.   Both cited in the *Oxford English dictionary*, 2nd ed., 1989.

Electronic Broadsides

By a strange twist of fate, a once popular form of printed communication—the broadside—is taking on new life in the Internet invisible college. The world of electronic bulletin boards, lists (listservs), and the other confusing and often confused forms of instantaneous national and international communication is complicated, multidimensional, disorganized to the point of being chaotic, and daunting to the outsider. It has also revived the polemical art of the broadside. It is interesting semantically to note that communication of these electronic broadsides is known as "posting."

If one looks at a vigorous and frequently literate listserv such as PACS-L (with its astonishing 8,900 members in more than 40 countries), one finds lots of little squibs, statements of fact and opinion, questions and answers, personal attacks; the kind of thing that (in another reference to a bygone age) is known as water-cooler talk. In addition, one finds assertive, sometimes thoughtful, often coherent statements of principle or on a particular issue—in other words, electronic broadsides.

Broadsides are easy to spot, particularly in retrospect. They tend to begin or advance threads of discussion or move those discussions in a different direction. They are also quoted heavily, both in direct responses or in contributions on related themes. They are also often misquoted and misinterpreted; something that has always been true of broadsides. Many are longer and more carefully written than the typical contribution—they give the sense of being composed off the network and not off the cuff.

There are a couple of ways in which electronic broadsides compare unfavorably with their print predecessors, but they also have a number of advantages. Electronic broadsides lack the typographical range and elegance of the best of the print versions, although they also lack the typographic horrors of some of today's more deranged leaflets and posters. Their use is also restricted to the electronic elite who have access to the Internet and other resources; that elite is growing in numbers but is far from being a true mass movement. A printed broadside could reach, theoretically, all the people in a given area and few outside that area. An electronic broadside can reach people all over the world but not all the people in any one area.

The advantages of the electronic broadside are many and, for the elite, convincing. First, the electronic broadside is legal and one's effort goes into its creation, not its distribution. Today's print broadsides are primarily distributed by hand as leaflets, since it is illegal (or severely restricted) in most jurisdictions to post printed matter on walls, telephone poles, and the like. Second, electronic broadsides provide the nearest to instant gratification that most of us see in this vale of tears. Responses, pro and con (and for many the gratification is equal in either case) can be received within hours or, at the most, a day or two. This was rarely the case, outside revolutions, for the author of a print broadside. Third, responses can not only be posted as readily as the original message, they (and the re-responses) can be tracked and linked into threads of discussion, something that was only possible in a very limited way (the community bulletin board) in the use of print broadsides.

Electronic Journals

The current (fourth) edition of the *Directory of electronic journals, newsletters, and academic discussion lists*[10] contains listings of thousands of electronic journals, newsletters, and discussion lists. The titles of the journals range from the *Bryn Mawr Classical Review* to *Dateline: Starfleet*. Reading the entries, one is struck by the difficulty of defining exactly what an electronic journal *is* and the engagingly ad hoc and volunteerist nature of most of the titles listed. In her foreword to the third edition of the directory, the editor addresses the problem of definition:

> Those who compile and publish a directory like to think they can see overarching trends. Two are worth mentioning: (1) blurring boundaries between the different types of electronic serial, so that it is difficult to categorize them by the same taxonomies as those used for paper serials; and, (2) blurring

---

10. Washington, D.C.: Association of Research Libraries, 1994.

boundaries between formats. That is, some electronic serials are electronic only, but various of them either index or review paper publications, and others move between electronic and more traditional formats. Some electronic journals produce paper or microform spinoffs and some paper journals appear selectively in electronic form. Various paper publishers are beginning to produce tables of contents or abstracts in advance electronically.[11]

The plain fact is that the definition of an electronic journal is difficult because the situation is murky. What libraries need— and what many have been predicting confidently for a long time—are electronic journals with the following characteristics: affordability, authority, coherence, consistency, copyright protection, and longevity. It is not good enough to speak of how journal price escalation is destroying the economies of libraries and then to propose the electronic journal as an answer. First we must consider the practicalities of a feasible electronic journal industry.

Writings on the topic of electronic journals are noted for the intellectual elision by which they move from stating the problem to proposing the answer—the electronic journal— without explaining how to get there. In a brief review of a conference on journals and scholarly communication held at the University of Chicago, John Maddox stated breezily "the notion that full-blown electronic journals will soon be multiplying was taken for granted, although the question of just when that will be is still open."[12] Indeed. That time is not now, given that most electronic journals listed in the *Directory*[13] are free, peer reviewed (if at all) in name only, and the product of unpaid individual effort. Such is not the basis for an enduring industry, especially as their distribution is dependent on free and freely available access to the Internet—a state of affairs that may not long endure.

---

11. Ann Okerson, Foreword to *Directory of electronic journals, newsletters, and academic discussion lists,* 3rd ed., Washington, D.C.: Association of Research Libraries, 1993, pp. i–ii.

12. John Maddox, "Electronic journals have a future," *Nature* 356 (April 16, 1992), p. 559.

13. *Directory of electronic journals... .*

There are some quarter of a million current serial titles in the world. They and the articles that appear in them are published for a variety of reasons—commercial and scholarly, venal and noble. Their costs rise all the time and libraries have all but given up on being able to deal with the serial anxiety that contemplation of them induces. That anxiety is particularly evident in the field of scientific, technical, and medical (STM) journals.

Library after library has looked on in horror as the price of STM journals has gone through the roof and subscriptions to them have only been maintained by cannibalizing the funds for other library materials. The long-predicted, long-anticipated advent of electronic journals is seen as a savior for libraries concerned with STM fields. Will it really be the solution or merely another mirage in the endless serial desert? In an otherwise positive piece, Jamie Cameron poses four as yet unanswered questions to journal publishers concerning their possible electronic future:

- ♦ Will electronic journals fulfill the current assessment role of print journals?

- ♦ How long will governments subsidize networks?

- ♦ How will funding patterns change?

- ♦ How are journal publishers to make money out of document delivery?[14]

The questions concern money and authority. Cameron quotes the judge in the *Texaco* case to great effect: "The profit motive is the engine that ensures the progress of science."[15] The judge was referring to the fact that uncontrolled photocopying of copyright materials could, in the end, lead to the demise of

---

14. Jamie Cameron, "The changing scene in journal publishing," *Publishers Weekly*, May 31, 1993, pp. 23–24.

15. Evan St. Lifer, "Publishers of science journals win copyright fair use ruling," *Library Journal* 117 (September 1, 1992), p. 110.

serial publishing but might as well have been referring to a far wider central issue, that of compensation for effort.

Our present system of journal publishing, defective though it may be, ensures rewards to publishers for publishing, writers for writing, and editors for editing. The rewards may be financial or they may be less tangible—recognition, promotion, tenure, meeting the collective goals of a learned society, etc.—but they are there and they are ensured in the print-on-paper journal publishing industry. For all the airy talk, there is no guarantee that a system of electronic journal publishing would yield those rewards and, thus, fuel the engine that drives progress in science and all other fields.

For the moment, the Internet is freely available to millions, most of whom are shielded from its actual costs by their institutions. If Internet support moves toward metered and restricted use, how many of today's "free" electronic journals would survive? If they did, and if a "subscriber" were free to excerpt, adapt, and retransmit any and all of the articles in an electronic journal, how would the interests of publishers and authors be protected?

Perhaps the whole idea of a "journal" as an assemblage of articles on related topics will pass away and each article contributed to the network will sink or swim on its own merits. When one considers the staggering numbers of photocopies, faxes, and digital transmissions of articles, it is evident that there is already a huge trade in the individual parts of journals, but that trade is piggybacking on the print journal industry. If each article was separate, how would a refereeing process work? How would the authors receive the tangible and intangible rewards of authorship? How would the authority of an author's intellectual property be protected? Who would create the massive indexing structure necessary to ensure access to "published" pieces? What would happen to articles that were "published" and never read? Who would preserve articles for posterity? These are major questions and they deserve more serious attention than they have yet received.

Looking for New Forms

The talk is of virtual libraries delivered to the average house-hold by the Baby Bells for $20 a month. Such a system would not be a "library" by any stretch of the imagination but a relatively modest information system. Is there a market for such a service at the cost of three or four paperback books a month?

So the search for new forms of electronic publishing and distribution goes on—a search that, when it descends from the world of fantasy, runs headlong into dull practical concerns such as copyright, economics, readability, demand, and loom-ing threats of government control. Until the major role that electronics have to play in the dissemination of *information* and the minor role in the dissemination of *knowledge* are clearly understood, the search will be fitful and unproductive and the dreams will remain with the dreamers while the rest of us get on with our lives.

Points to Remember

📖   Some publications primarily concerned with information and data should be replaced by electronic distribution.

📖   Proposals made for CD-ROM publications for the mass market have proved to be infeasible.

📖   Grandiose schemes for massive online text databases do not work.

📖   The Internet is the "invisible college" of old carried on by new means. It has revitalized the art of the broadside.

📖   Electronic journals work in certain limited areas and are a valuable addition to the mix.

5

Coping with Electronic Information

Knowledge may well be power. But knowledge is not the same as information and we should not confuse these two things. What we are seeing is an information explosion but we can have all the information in the world and be totally powerless unless we have the ability to analyse and interpret this mass of data.

Suzanne Moore

Communication technology has always had Procrustean tendencies. Through the years, some have assumed that the dominant technology of the moment is *the* answer for all kinds of communication and have cramped and distorted the general view of communication by that assumption. When the dominant means of distributing text and images was print, everything looked like a possible book, pamphlet, newspaper, magazine, or poster. The advent of radio led to radio doctors, radio propaganda, radio plays, teaching by radio, and so on. Then came television—still considered in some quarters to be the only answer to the problems of communication in a complex world. We cannot afford universities, so what is the answer? Why, distance learning[1]—in which interactive television

---

1.   This unlovely, ungrammatical phrase seems to have been translated literally from the German. In English it would, of course, be "distant learning" or, better, "distant teaching."

is the mode of transmission. Some will even assert that distance learning is *better* than classroom instruction. It should not be surprising that the same process is at work when it comes to electronic media.

At this stage of intellectual evolution, people should be able to accept the ambiguities and complexity of many and diverse means of communication. More, it should not be difficult to make decisions on which medium is better in a given case based on reason rather than ideology. Alas, little changes and we still confront the mentality that believes *all* electronic communication is better than all other means.

Many texts and other sources of data and information make more sense when transmitted by means of CD-ROM or online access than they do as books. It is possible that we will discover an increasing number of such publications. The relative future proportion of print (and other linear) publications and of electronic publications is a matter of no philosophical importance. Not only is it unimportant, it cannot be predicted and the surest sign of an electronic snake-oil merchant is the confident statement about how much of the market will be occupied by electronic publications in, say, 2010. The important theoretical and practical point is that we recognize and welcome the multiplicity of means of communication and the strengths and weaknesses of each.

Print-on-paper has *never* been the best medium for many kinds of data and information. The legitimate promise of electronic publishing is to provide better (that is, cheaper, more ecologically sound, more up-to-date, easier) access to *certain kinds* of text—replacing books and journals where books and journals have never worked very well. Librarians would have been foolish to ignore this promise of electronic publishing and—despite the accusations of some futurists—they have *not* been so foolish. Librarians and publishers/distributors should work together to ensure that the promise of electronic publishing continues to be realized, that real economies in library budgets can be made, and that the various forms of electronic publishing are used intelligently and appropriately.

Despite its many advantages for transmitting and giving access to data and some types of information, electronic publishing has inherent drawbacks in addition to those discussed in earlier chapters. Simply dealing with the practical problems of electronic sources can be difficult. These may include locating the desired information, determining the appropriateness of what is found, and knowing whether what is found is authentic (i.e., is what it says it is)—none of which is easily overcome. Then there are the issues of using electronic texts that go beyond readability itself (discussed in Chapter 2) that can be summarized as: Can the user cope with the quantity and lack of structure of the data and information?

Data, Information, Knowledge

We have previously discussed the definitions of, and differences between, **data**, **information**, and **knowledge**. Many people appear unwilling to concede that data and information are not the sum of human communication. Data and small assemblages of information are readily amenable to electronic transmission and access. Complex aggregations of information and recorded knowledge are not so amenable—that is a fact with which proponents of an all-electronic future have failed to deal.

Those proponents, in hot pursuit of electronic everything, tell us that the world's information (or the world's knowledge or something like that) is doubling every five years. They go on to argue that only electronic methods can possibly keep up with such a massive increase. It may well be true that the volume of *data* in the world is doubling every five years. That is not at all the same as saying that the amount of information or knowledge is increasing at such a rate.

Thirty years ago, Yehoshua Bar-Hillel inveighed against those pushing the "flood-of-information" theory.[2] It is a pity that his trenchant analyses of the situation have not changed the tenor of the discussion, which is still pervaded by extreme statements about an "information explosion" (more exactly, a "data explosion" or even a "document explosion") requiring electronic solutions.

---

2.   Yehoshua Bar-Hillel, *Language and information*, Reading, Mass.: Addison-Wesley, 1964.

It is almost certainly nonsense to say that the amount of *useful* information is doubling every five years. A cynic might even suggest that the amount of knowledge is *declining*, as so many people seem caught up in pursuing more and more data, failing to turn it into either useful information or worthwhile knowledge. Libraries and human communication in general are, and should be, more concerned with knowledge and what it leads to and should not be diverted by irrelevant discussions of a supposed crisis calling for electronic, and only electronic, solutions.

Data overload is nothing new. For example, every day insurance companies churn out immense quantities of paper containing new or modified policies and coverage descriptions; more than any person could read or evaluate. Virtually none of it is relevant to anyone but the company and its clients; virtually none of it belongs on a library's shelves or in its electronic resources; and virtually none of it contributes to the knowledge of humankind or enriches our culture. These are not value judgments. The data may very well be commercially useful and necessary, but it should be seen for what it is—unprocessed data and, as such, of little concern to libraries.

Coping with the I-Way

Electronic distribution, both of data and of information, will certainly continue to grow rapidly. There is little question that the I-way (or Information Superhighway) now being developed on the basis of the Internet will be a major conduit for, and source of, data and information in the coming years. It is obvious that more data and information will be distributed electronically than in print by the end of the century; that may well be true now. Beyond the "gee whiz" aspects of this trend lie some rather difficult questions. The most problematic is: what do we do with all that *stuff*?

More data means more dross and more difficulty in locating the gold—the information that is relevant and useful. It is by no means clear that anyone has developed reasonable strategies for coping with massive amounts of electronic data or that the funding is available for such reasonable strategies to be devised. Moreover, those strategies, even if they existed, would be focused on data and discrete packages of information. The task of providing ways for the I-way user to use full texts efficiently and productively is far more difficult.

Organization

Full-text databases, whether as part of a global nightmare such as Project Xanadu or in more local and manageable contexts, require new and complex retrieval techniques. Advocates of online everything can be surprisingly casual about the need for, and present lack of, the ways to deal with large accumulations of electronic texts.

One simplistic suggestion is "use string searching to find what you want." There are three major problems with that approach. First, it assumes that the words chosen by the user will lead to a significant proportion of the relevant paragraphs. Students of indexing will remember the concepts of "recall"—the proportion of relevant materials retrieved—and "relevance"—the degree to which retrieved materials match the desired outcome. These ideas are vital to the understanding of the use of electronic texts. Second, this approach assumes that the searching will be fast enough to be acceptable and useful. Third, and most significantly, it assumes that the user can handle the results in terms of volume and structure. It can readily be predicted that for large full-text databases almost any single word will yield far too many paragraphs for the average user—to say nothing of what happens when a "smart" search system automatically searches for synonyms as well.

It is entirely possible that there is *no* universal solution for truly massive full-text databases—that is, a solution that allows the user to treat the entire collection of material as a single searchable entity and hope to make effective use of the results. Large full-text databases are very effective ways of losing information and knowledge in vast swamps of unorganized data, and the dangers they pose to the student and the researcher should not be ignored or underestimated.

None of this means that full texts of some items should not be available electronically. Textual analysis is a significant scholarly tool. We are not scholars enough to understand its strengths and weaknesses, but there is no doubt that the computer can simplify the process and make certain kinds of analysis possible.[3] Many texts really do work at a paragraph-by-paragraph level, and such texts (reference works being the obvious example) are more usable when made available in electronic form.

Is WAIS the Answer?

One solution to the full-text searching dilemma that is being touted on the Internet these days is WAIS (Wide-Area Information Servers). WAIS has been shown to work in test cases, but those test cases are almost always fairly modest, and the reports on the tests are really rather sketchy.

The original WAIS ranks citations by weighted word occurrence—but each word in the search is considered equivalent. Thus, an item with 80 occurrences of "war" and none of "civil" is actually considered much more relevant than an item with five occurrences of the phrase "Civil War."

A more sophisticated WAIS looks at word density (the percentage of an article that consists of the requested words). Common sense suggests that relevance ranking based on word density will tend to lead users to brief overviews and digests more than to key articles or detailed discussions. Such ranking could fairly be dubbed *USA Today* retrieval or Retrieval Lite.

The more advanced the text-retrieval system and the larger the full-text database, the more dependent the user is on the internal workings of the system. The user will not be aware of what is happening and must trust that he or she is being given the "most relevant" items. Moreover, with gigabytes of text in even a small full-text database, there is no way that user can know differently.

Those who advocate WAIS assert that it will work effectively on a full-text database of up to 30 gigabytes. If that sounds large, it is—but, to put it in context, it is the equivalent of 30,000 to 50,000 books: the contents of a medium-sized branch library, the kind of collection that is easily navigated. The key to successful electronic dissemination is sheer quantity; a year's

---

3.   See, for example: David L. Wilson, "Creating electronic texts," *Chronicle of Higher Education*, June 15, 1994.

worth of text will certainly be far more than 30 gigabytes. WAIS is, therefore, a system that works as well as it can in the kind of full-text database that is no improvement over a well-organized collection of books with indexes. We are still left with the dilemma of massive full-text databases that are, in essence, unusable.

Will Full-Text Searching in Very Large Databases Ever Work?

Those who have tried to use many of the resources on the Internet by a variety of access techniques, other than those who are emotionally committed to the technology, will have mixed feelings about searching truly large databases, particularly distributed full-text databases. What takes a minute to find in ABI/Inform may take hours to find using Gopher, Archie, WAIS, and the like, if the search meets with any success at all.

That should not be surprising. After all, a substantial amount of up-front intellectual effort has gone into ABI/Inform to create brief, searchable abstracts. For legal reasons, those abstracts cannot be available as "free" Internet resources. The latter means the Internet user must search the raw text instead—not a fast or necessarily feasible option.

Tools other than those currently available have been suggested, up to and including "virtual information realities," by means of which scholars will somehow visualize the sphere of data and then home in visually on the peaks of interest to them. Such a vision may have a skewed, daffy charm, but it presumes incalculable amounts of advance organization of raw materials *and* that meaningful virtual-reality constructs are achievable. To date, most dream examples rely on truly impressive feats of structuring, a kind of organization of which no computer is currently capable.

There is no real reason to believe that any conceivable computer could determine the *meaning* of text, the *relative significance* of an article to any given field, or any other critical aspect of retrieval. Meaning cannot be determined by word counts or density of phraseology, and the processes of the human mind cannot be reduced to bean counting. The fact that such visions are in the discussion at all argues a certain desperation on the part of futurists confronted with a problem that, in their secret hearts, they know may not be solvable.

Bibliographic and Quality Control

There are professionals in this country who have developed very effective means of bringing huge quantities of records of information and knowledge under control and making their retrieval possible. That group was one of the earliest to use computers for everyday tasks, and has used computers with increasing effectiveness for at least three decades. Amazingly, given that the group is consistently underfunded and incredibly disparate, they managed to come up with an innovative data management design more than a quarter-century ago, a design that has supported cost-effective systems handling tens of gigabytes of data covering tens of millions of records.

Unfortunately, that group—professional librarians—tends to be ignored by the computer wizards dreaming of new and wonderful tools. Worse, some librarians seem to ignore their own achievements and assume that the new ways, even ways that exist only in the fertile brain of some futurist, are better. It is likely that librarians are the only group with the professional qualifications, experience, and track record to make them capable of bringing quality, structure, and bibliographic control to the global rats' nest that is the Internet. Librarians have the professional training and experience; many have specific training in the technological environment; and they have simply done a better job of organizing the world of knowledge and information than anyone else. Despite all this, librarians are routinely castigated for being technologically retrograde. The facts belie this accusation. Librarians have been using computers effectively to provide real, but never total or permanent, solutions to incredibly complex problems since the early 1960s. Librarians have used lower-technology solutions to make sense of multimillion-volume book collections enriched by other media. Librarians have done better at making sense of massive quantities of disparate information than any other group. It is a proud record; one to build on, not one to forget.

Authenticity

How can the user of an electronic resource be sure that the electronic text received is identical to the text requested? If the user has requested an electronic text based on a citation, how can he or she be sure that the text received is the one that was cited? How can the user be sure that the text received is in fact the text that was created by the person named as its author? How can the user be sure that the person named as author is the creator of the text? In short, how can the authenticity of the text be guaranteed in an electronic environment?

A number of people say these questions do not matter—that a big advantage of electronic texts is that they are mutable, constantly being updated and revised. This may be a good thing for some kinds of data and purely factual information. In order for the mutability not to be significant, the user must know that the source can be trusted and that history is irrelevant.

A user following up a citation needs to know that the article he or she is reading is the article as it was when it was cited. At the very least, if it is not exactly that article but the author's current version, or one that has been changed by another person, the fact that the article has been changed (and ideally the changes themselves) should be clearly indicated. For one thing, a well-written article is much more than a series of facts. Readers derive information from data and knowledge from information; that process is debased if the reader is presented with knowledge and information that has been "improved" by anonymous others. The situation is even worse when the reader is unaware that the deformation of the text has taken place.

There are solutions to the problem of authenticity in electronic texts. Currently, the easiest is to write the text to a read-only medium; in other words, to publish it on CD-ROM. Another is to prepare a "checksum," a digital signature that can verify that the text has almost certainly not been modified. The technology exists to create such a security measure; at this point, the will to do so is lacking.

Today, most electronic texts simply cannot claim the same validity or importance as printed texts. This must change, given the reality of modern communication and the economics of communication. Electronic distribution *must* complement print-on-paper and each must be used in the manner that yields the best results. To do that effectively, a battery of solutions must be found for the many problems of electronic distribution. A necessary precursor of these solutions is abandoning the idea that "putting it on the net" solves everything—or solves anything, for that matter.

Significance

Internetters made much of a recent *New Yorker* cartoon with the caption "On the Internet, nobody knows you're a dog."[4] The joke is based on one of the wonders of electronic communication—it has no inherent discrimination on the basis of age, creed, color, gender, physical appearance or ability, or sexual preference. That is entirely to the good.

It seems to go further than that, though. An equally relevant cartoon could have the caption "On the Internet, nobody knows you're a crank." Internet users know that the Net does not exclude those who are ignorant or bigoted, cannot write a simple declarative English sentence, or have neglected to check their facts. Sadly, many electronic messages emanate from cranks and fools (they seem to have a lot more time than the rest of us). We can only trust that the sunshine of scrutiny will enable discrimination between the wheat and the tares.

Is it possible for users of electronic texts to judge significance and quality with any assurance? How can they estimate the likelihood that a given text is either correct or useful? In the print world, those familiar with a given discipline can make first-level decisions based on the source. For example, everyone in a field knows the top-ranked journals in that field and gives more credence to articles published in those journals than to articles published in totally unknown journals. That credence and ranking may be one of the greatest problems faced by those who would reform scholarly journal publishing—how do you change the rankings?

Where are the top-ranked electronic sources? How does a user determine whether a paragraph on a given topic is important, current, or even correct? Should the history of World War

---

4. *New Yorker*, July 5, 1993, p. 61.

II be studied in an arena in which the works of "Holocaust revisionists" appear to have the same standing as the works of mainstream historians?

These are important questions—ones that librarians must answer daily in choosing and using print materials. The questions become much more difficult (if not impossible) to answer in an electronic environment. If those questions are not answered, electronic dissemination will continue to be less significant than print, if only because it is so much more difficult to evaluate what the user is getting.

Drowning, Surfing, or Swimming in the Sea of Information

As we have noted, large insurance companies generate huge quantities of data on paper. Most of that data is also in machine-readable form. Let us imagine that a scholar wishes to study the insurance industry and manages to gain access to all that machine-readable data. Let us also stipulate that the scholar has access to all the computer resources she or he can possibly use. What will the scholar's options be? Most probably, that scholar will end up drowning in data—and there's a good possibility that no useful information will ever emerge from the flood. Unless, of course, the scholar has the insight and inspiration to establish incredibly efficient ways of reducing that data to information—ways that a computer can carry out unaided. Even if that unlikely scenario were so, what if another scholar doubts the results and determines to go back to the raw materials? Good luck—we'll see you in a few decades!

That may be an extreme case but it is not unrealistic. Why is it, then, that so many people today seem determined to drown in data and information, spending so much time taking it all in that they never have time to synthesize knowledge and achieve understanding?

It is very easy to drown in information even now. The rapid expansion of full-text resources—which *will* happen—will greatly increase the dangers of drowning.[5] Futurists tell us that a "knowbot" (*know*ledge ro*bot*—a species of electronic librarian) will handle retrieval for us, operating throughout the nets and sending us whatever is relevant to our interests. Leaving aside the whiff of the 1939 World's Fair that clings to this concept, there are two important, unanswered questions about knowbots. How can a computer program judge relevance in a meaningful, useful way? Given a reasonable breadth of interest, how can the knowbot be stopped from drowning the user in material (relevant and irrelevant)?

The Young Scholar's Peril

We are told that any reputable scholar must be up-to-date on everything in his or her field (which will, these days, be quite narrowly defined). Taking that admonition literally and using electronic tools to achieve it is a recipe for disaster. Young scholars who make it a point of pride to keep absolutely up-to-the-minute on every available piece of information in their field will find at least one of two things happening:

♦ They will define their field so narrowly, and build search tools that search so restrictively, that they will miss the most important work being done in the field and become irrelevant.

♦ They will spend so much time (and money) keeping up with developments that there will never be time to organize, analyze, synthesize—in other words, *create*.

Some assert that, in the future, all scholarship will be cooperative and iterative and that this is to the good. This assertion is oversimplified to the point of inanity. Some scholarship is, and should be, cooperative. Much of the best new thinking, however, is not. Some scholarship arises out of simply massaging existing data. Much of the best, however, depends on stepping back, viewing the field anew, and bringing individual genius to

---

5.   For a discussion of the effects of too much unstructured information, see: Richard Saul Wurman, *Information anxiety*, New York: Doubleday, 1989.

bear. Those who are drowning in information will be hard-pressed to take part in the former variety of scholarship and there seems to be no way that they can do the latter. For that, they will need to learn to disconnect from The Net, recognize that they will miss some items in the field, and sit back and think. Reflection is an honorable activity, but hard to do while drowning.

Surfing

The metaphor of the sea for the Internet is pervasive and illuminating. When one thinks of the uncharted depths, the innumerable varieties of aquatic life, and the dangers to life and happiness posed by the sea, the metaphor is irresistible. Even the sunnier applications of the metaphor have resonance. Surfing, after all, consists of skimming the surface in search of superficial and transitory pleasure. The surfing analogy is nothing new and "Surfing the Internet" has been worked to death as a title for courses and articles. Surfing is skimming over the Sea of Information; maneuvering without getting in too deeply—a quite different matter from being aware of all available resources and how to find them.

Surfing is an essential skill for anyone who wishes to become an effective user of electronic texts. However, it is scarcely unique to the Internet or other electronic structures. We know there has always been journal surfing: skimming through vast realms of information without getting bogged down by attempting to study each item in detail. Some people are better journal surfers than others, but most learn to be fairly proficient in those areas where they have to be *somewhat* familiar with what is current but cannot afford to spend all their waking hours at it.

A literary scholar might regard two or three journals and magazines as fundamental to her or his own interests. That scholar will probably subscribe to those publications and read them cover to cover. A committed person will have wider interests and, given time and access to a good collection, may well look at twenty or more other journals. For most of those journals (say 80 percent) "looking" will consist of glancing at the contents page in the expectation that one article every three or four years might be worth reading. For a smaller number of journals (most of the remaining 20 percent), the reader will glance at the abstract or first paragraph of each article and skim through the book reviews, probably reading a significant portion of each issue. That leaves a few core journals—the ones read in full. This description is another form of the 80/20 rule—20 percent of an area represents 80 percent of the value. The key element to such surfing is knowing which 20 percent deserves extra attention. Beyond that, the journal surfer needs flexibility in recognizing that important articles may occur in the lightly skimmed majority.

Is it possible to apply print journal surfing techniques to the electronic sea? It can be, but remember that it is one thing to skim a set of article titles in an electronic source; it is quite another to request the abstract for each one (particularly as the cost of doing so will increase as we move beyond our present fully-subsidized era), and it is yet another to want to look at each article.

Surfing can take place at several levels. Skimming through tables of contents of many different journals is quite different from having a highly selective search routine running on a computer. In the first case, the reader is aware of all those paper names, thus acquiring a sense of what is being published, which in turn helps to foster awareness of trends. That process is a form of socialization. It is also one reason that so many areas have at least one key journal or bulletin, a journal that many or most people in the field actually *read* in full (every issue, more-or-less cover to cover) as part of keeping up with the field. This type of surfing adds considerably more value than most Internet surfing. It is also more time consuming and, in a way, more random. It is hard to see it as being readily transferable to the electronic domain.

Swimming

Some people seem to be full-time surfers—always aware of today's currents of information and how to find enough to keep them happy, but never deeply conversant with any particular current. Some of these electronic beach bums become deeply involved in the e-mail culture—true creatures of the network.

In extreme cases, if something is not on the Net and available via one of their news groups or lists, it either does not exist or its existence is without significance.

Luckily, most people cease to surf and become swimmers, at least from time to time and place to place. Swimmers read whole articles; the more advanced even read books! They explore topics in detail, not only connecting article to article but idea to idea. As this process unfolds, the swimmer will frequently move to the next step, by adding to the topics through analysis, synthesis, further research—creation. This is when it gets good.

For the Internet user, the problem is knowing the difference between swimming, surfing, and drowning. The important factor is attitude. A swimmer who becomes obsessed with currency and completeness will soon drown. If the user finds that she or he no longer reads complete articles in an area, that is surfing—not necessarily a bad thing, but one that indicates relative priorities and relative awareness.

We envisage the successful scholar on the Net as both a swimmer and a surfer. Some surf too much—treating all books as being outdated by definition; ignoring all but the few leading journals in a specialty; or, worse, ignoring *all* journals and relying only on preprints, electronic mail, and personal communications. It is conceivable that such an approach might work in a few disciplines but it meets no present scholarly standard. A balance of surfing and swimming serves most users well in their attempts to cope with the electronic chaos of today. Unfortunately, the tools for surfing and swimming effectively do not yet exist—we have no complete and accurate charts for the Sea of Information. We hope that such tools can and will be developed, and repeat our conviction that librarians are the most competent to develop them.

Points to Remember

📖 The world's total data may double every five years, but no evidence suggests such increases for the world's information or knowledge.

📖 No known tools will support effective searching of very large heterogeneous full-text databases.

📖 Librarians have done better at making sense of huge, heterogeneous databases than any other group, and should continue to do so in the future.

📖 Users of electronic publications must be able to assure the authenticity of such publications—easy with CD-ROM, more difficult with electronic distribution.

📖 Effective users of electronic resources must learn to surf the networks and, on occasion, to swim in information without drowning in data.

6

Deconstructing Dreams of the All-Electronic Future

L ibraries and librarians face a multiplicity of difficult problems in dealing with their collections and resources (in print and other media). Naturally, those problems have a variety of possible solutions and, the world being what it is, the problems and solutions change. This state of affairs is unacceptable to many writers and theoreticians who react by lumping a complex of related problems into a single problem—one to which they promise a single grand solution. That grand solution is, of course, inevitable, at least to those who project it. Here is a quick, not entirely impartial, summary of their thinking:

♦ All data, information, and recorded knowledge on all subjects will be available at all times and all locations. Access will be by universal workstation, wireless personal digital assistant, networked personal computer, or home infotainment center.

♦ Everyone will be able to make effective use of all this data and information. Everyone will consider this to be the only way to deal with texts, graphics, numbers, and other material. Everyone will gladly pay the small sums demanded for all of this. Problems of copyright, authority of texts and graphics, organization, filtering, intellectual property rights, and the like are just potholes on the golden road of progress and will soon and easily be solved.

♦ Libraries will cease to exist as physical entities at about the same time print ceases to exist as a medium of publication and distribution. A few may print texts from their infotainment centers but that practice, too, will end. Some libraries may still be around in the form of rooms containing subsidized terminals for those few who cannot afford their own personal stations, but those "libraries" too shall pass when we are in the Universal Electronic Information Age.

♦ In the short period before the triumph of electronic information, libraries will stop worrying about maintaining local collections of non-electronic materials and learn to give access to material at the time at which it is needed. Someone else (unnamed) will maintain and, better yet, pay for the collections to which access will be given.

This "vision" is an irresponsible, illogical, and unworkable nightmare. It is cartoonish in that it suggests a future that is much simpler than the present—a future in which all problems disappear as if by magic. It is, like most fantasies, an escape from reality and not a serious attempt to deal with the world as it really is.

The Information Marketplace

Advocates of the universal electronic vision hold that people will soon find electronic access so superior to old-fashioned print-on-paper, *for all uses of print*, that print will simply wither and die. Witness:

The publishing industry will be totally electronic from production to distribution.

For academic information purposes the book will, eventually, become solely of antiquarian or aesthetic interest.

If one does not accept these basic tenets then one is not facing reality.[1]

This nonsensical marketplace argument is essentially harmless unless it is used to make investment decisions or accepted by powerful and gullible people. Some university administrations and public library boards have already been influenced in their decisions on libraries because they have accepted the All-Electronic Future without question.

The Universal Workstation

University administrators dream of the Universal Workstation, decreasingly called the Scholar's Workstation—perhaps because of the ridicule the name induced. Computer makers dream of the personal digital assistant and of the networked personal computer with access to everything, any time, and from anywhere. Futurists contemplating the media and entertainment fields dream of the home infotainment center with similar access. Visions of dollar signs dance in their heads. By whatever name, these dreams are of the universal workstation—a device that provides instant access to everything anyone ever wishes or needs to see, hear, or read.

An effective universal workstation must pass several modest tests in order to make sense for users and for society:

♦ **Availability:** Everything that has ever been recorded (printed, photographed, filmed, taped, painted, drawn, etc.) must be converted to, or created in, digital form in order to be available to the universal workstation user.

---

1.   Mel W. Collier, Anne Ramsden, and Zimin Wu, "The electronic library: virtually a reality," in *Opportunity 2000: 15th International Essen Symposium*, Essen: Universitatsbibliothek Essen, 1993, pp. 135–146.

♦ **Findability and appropriateness** (our old friends "recall" and "relevance"): Each user of the universal workstation must be able to find all relevant electronic documents in this digital universe rapidly and easily. A user must be able to determine the relevance of retrieved electronic documents based on her or his personal needs and preferences.

♦ **Authenticity:** Each user must be confident that retrieved electronic documents displayed at the universal workstation are authentic—that is, they are what was originally created and they are what was asked for.

♦ **Usability:** Each electronic document retrieved must be available in a form that makes it usable on each user's workstation and be at least as easy and pleasant to use as documents in the earlier media that have been replaced.

♦ **Protection of intellectual property:** Each document retrievable at the universal workstation must be made available in a manner that protects intellectual property rights and ensures proper and prompt remuneration to the author.

♦ **Affordability:** The true costs of providing needed and wanted portions of the digital universe must be reasonable. At least, the total economic and ecological costs of providing digital access should be no higher than the comparable costs of providing traditional equivalents.

Not one of these criteria can be met today. There is little chance that *any* of them can be met in any foreseeable future. Without these criteria, no universal workstation; without the universal workstation, no glorious All-Electronic Future. In truth, the universal workstation is not an appropriate goal because it can never be a universal replacement for print and other analog media.

The key point here is *replacement*. It is no accident that some futurists will not contemplate the print and electronic media in peaceful coexistence. The economic case for the universal workstation rests squarely on abandoning well-maintained print collections. If sound print collections are maintained *and* work proceeds toward a universal workstation, the objection to the model becomes that it simply requires more resources than are available. *That mixed model is not affordable.*

Digital workstations cannot provide access to the primary record—manuscripts, printed materials, paintings, drawings, etc., in their original form. Does that matter? It may not to the mass of people but it does to many scholars.[2] The interest in primary records appears to be growing in the scholarly community and should not be dismissed because it is a minority concern. To ignore the need for the primary record is to deny a substantial aspect of scholarship and, thus, to weaken the role of the humanities even further.

Universal Access and Universal Conversion

Most documents are not in electronic form. If one leaves aside the mountains of unorganized electronic data, perhaps less than 5 percent of the world's recorded knowledge and information is available in digital form. That percentage will increase but it is hard to imagine any entity or combination of entities putting up the mega-billions of dollars necessary to convert, say, 50 percent of extant documents (textual and graphic). Even futurists must come to terms with the idea that many things never will be in electronic form, particularly while they are in copyright. Just because something is not available electronically, it is not inherently unimportant except, perhaps, to a fringe of truly devoted electronic enthusiasts.

Even setting aside copyright and authenticity issues and the lack of adequate reading devices, conversion of print material is a slow and enormously expensive proposition, particularly if one takes the reasonable position that each electronic document should have, at least, all the attributes of the non-electronic document from which it was taken. This means not

---

2. Phyllis Franklin, "Scholars, librarians, and the future of primary records," *College & Research Libraries*, September 1993, pp. 397–406.

just the text of a *Book of Hours*, *PC Magazine*, or *New Yorker* but also the typography, layout, illustrations, advertisements, etc. To achieve that reasonable goal (why do it at all if the result is inferior?), conversion means high-resolution true-color scanning and retention of each page, as well as conversion of text to machine-readable form. If the originals are to be preserved, it will be a slow and labor-intensive process; if not, it will still be slow and expensive.

An honest advocate of the mass conversion of linear documents would admit that the cost of storage must continue to decline precipitously if such conversion is ever to be economic. A single 8-by-10-inch page image stored in full color, before data compression, will occupy approximately 86 megabytes of storage and at least 22 megabytes even after compression.[3] The July 25, 1994, issue of the *New Yorker* has 86 pages (they are slimmer in the summer) and would thus require about 7,430 megabytes before compression and 1,850 after. Then there is the scanning itself, and the conversion to text form for searching and analysis; optical character recognition is better than it was, but no responsible institution would rest the future of the human record on the assumption of 100 percent correct recognition without painstaking and expensive manual checks.

Real-World Examples

Continuing with the *New Yorker*—what would we need to convert, say, one year's worth? It would probably take at least a person-month (about 160 hours) under ideal conditions, and would require storage of something like 49 gigabytes (49,000 megabytes, 49 billion bytes) for each year, assuming compression down to 25 percent of original, and an average of 150 pages per issue: 30 color, 30 with gray-scale illustrations. The storage space taken also assumes that conversion is "intelligent," using the most efficient technique for each page. These estimates

---

3. Storage requirements are based on scanning at 600 dpi, almost certainly the lowest useful resolution for printed magazines, newspapers, and books, using 24-bit scans for full-color pages, 8-bit (256-gray-scale) scans for pages with noncolor art, and 1-bit scans for pure text pages. Compression to 25 percent of the original size, an optimistic figure, is assumed.

leave out time and space for converting text and providing indexing. If it is not possible to sense which pages require advanced conversion and no manual intervention is used, a lot more storage will be required—168 gigabytes per year, assuming true-color conversion of all 150 pages of each issue.

How about *PC Magazine* at 22 issues a year, averaging about 450 pages each (almost all with color)? Assuming compression to 25 percent of original, that is 9.7 gigabytes per issue (or about 213 per year) and another person-month to do the job. To put the storage into perspective, *two years* of *PC Magazine* will take more storage than The Research Libraries Group's primary databases! A complete run of the magazine through 1994 would require 2.8 terabytes. A terabyte is 1,000 gigabytes, so we are talking about almost *three trillion* characters.

Three terabytes is much more than the disk storage at OCLC—just to store a 13-year run of one magazine. But storage is practically free, right? Incidentally, a year of a typical metropolitan newspaper—80 pages daily, 300 pages Sunday, with color on 10 percent of daily pages and 50 percent of Sunday pages—will need around 1.5 terabytes of storage, assuming a 4-to-1 compression ratio.

What of other media? Purely visual media should be converted at even higher resolutions if the electronic visual document is to "equal" its non-electronic source. Recorded sound can be digitized readily, if it is accepted that current sampling levels actually capture everything that is on the original (many audio purists do not accept that they do). An hour of stereophonic sound captured at 44.1 kHz sampling frequency with 16-bit resolution requires roughly 450 megabytes—that is, a 600-megabyte CD holds roughly 75 minutes of music. Motion pictures present the same problems that apply to visual media and recorded sound—primarily, massive data storage requirements for accurate digitization.

Since video has much less information than film to begin with, it poses fewer problems; the storage requirements are still large, but not on the scale of film. Nevertheless, digitized video of American broadcast quality still requires one gigabyte for each *minute* of program, before compression. In other words, a two-hour film, reduced to broadcast quality, would require more than 200 CD-ROMs. Compression can reduce that considerably, but compression has its limits. Those who have seen video from CD-ROM will know what this means—typically, tiny portions of the screen displaying jerky images in an effort to produce an acceptable image within the constraints of the storage medium.

Selective Conversion: Who Decides?

No amount of handwaving, mumbo-jumbo, or blithe assumptions that the future will answer all problems can disguise the plain fact that society cannot afford anything even approaching universal conversion. We have not the money or time to do the conversion and cannot provide the storage. This is made clear by the description of the Library of Congress' ambitious Digital Library Project.[4] Ordinary book pages are expected to cost between $2 and $6 each to convert; the figures for rare and fragile materials and nontext media are much higher. Even if it is funded fully, the Project will convert one million *images* (not items) a year: the equivalent of 5,000 200-page books. If LC stopped acquiring books today, that would mean it would have converted 5 percent of its collection by the year 2216. Alternatively, it could convert 3 percent of its new acquisitions with neither time nor money for retrospective digitization.[5]

It will be argued that universal conversion is not necessary. Here is how that argument goes. Most magazines are so transient that they do not need to be converted and, in any case, all advertisements and other non-editorial matter can be left out. Who needs romance, science fiction, or mystery novels in electronic form? Who needs anything but the best and most up-to-date nonfiction works? The answer, surely, is that we only need to convert a tiny fraction of today's print publications.

This approach is a recipe for totalitarianism, a refined form of book-burning. Who will make the decisions? Ultimately, those with the gold make the rules and, in this case, that means the government and mega-business. Selective conversion ac-

---

4.   Peter H. Lewis, "Library of Congress offering to feed data superhighway," *New York Times*, September 12, 1994.

5.   See also James H. Billington, "Electronic content and civilization's discontent," *Educom Review* 29 (September/October 1994), pp. 22–25.

companied by denial of access to the unconverted material—after all, we cannot afford both the Great Electronic Database *and* real libraries—is a perilous policy indeed. Just to take one example, a person studying social history in the United States needs newspapers and popular magazines as source material, and the advertisements, typography, and illustrations are at least as important as the texts of articles.

The intellectual and social consequences of selective conversion are ghastly at best. Had that happened earlier, we would all be spared Charles Dickens. He, after all, was just the most popular author of his time, not the most respected. The same goes for the obscure Gregor Mendel and his crazy theories. Trash, all of it; let it decay in peace. In these enlightened times, we know what is good and right, do we not? It will surely simplify the history of scientific development to clear out all those false starts and side paths. Let us not convert any creationist or overly enthusiastic evolutionist works, for example. That way, future generations will know that the only acceptable truth is this decade's scientific view of evolution.

Diverse Selectivity

Each library selects, as does each reader. Each library selects and retains according to different criteria. The sheer cost and scale of electronic conversion will encourage and even force monolithic decision-making as to what gets converted. It will also run into another problem, one that also applies to newly created electronic materials. This problem needs to be considered carefully by those who advocate virtual libraries, universal workstations, and electronic everything. Namely, if libraries are dependent on retrieving the bulk of resources from elsewhere, who controls the repositories? How many repositories will there be? Tom Vogl noted:

> As virtual libraries are created, there will be increased pressure on hard-copy libraries to relinquish their precious space and with it their physical collections, in whole or in part. Inevitably, both the soft and hard copies will be extant in fewer and fewer places, in a few well endowed libraries in hard copy and on a relatively few hard disks, all clearly identified as to location. Such a potential for thought control and effective book burning

has not existed since Gutenberg, or possibly since the burning of the library at Alexandria.[6]

Those who believe that money and time are available for comprehensive conversion might also be persuaded to believe that government entities would never, ever think of rewriting history, concealing information, or in some other manner interfering with the cultural record.

The Ecology of the All-Electronic Future

Advocates of the all-electronic future and virtual libraries say that one of the reasons why print publishing should cease is so we can stop "cutting down all those trees."[7] Extreme advocates speak movingly of first-growth redwoods and rain forests while ignoring the reality that most paper is either recycled or made from "trash trees"—fast-growing trees farmed for just that purpose—and that high quality paper can be made from almost any fiber, including kudzu[8] and other worthless plants.

Let us consider whether electronic distribution will, in fact, save paper, at least within library settings. It is evident most people will insist on paper copies of texts more than 100 lines long—all books and most articles. In an all-electronic world, this means that each text will be printed each time it is to be read—at the relatively high cost of local printers. Someone taking the text of a 6-by-9-inch book, printed on both sides, and printing it on one side of 8.5-by-11-inch paper, will use about three times as much paper *for that copy*.

As a national average, each book in a public library goes out 2.5 times a year. Thus, printing on demand, whether done in the library or at home, would consume 7.5 times as much paper *each year* as is held in all our public libraries. That is not

---

6.   Tom Vogl, electronic message on PACS-L, February 20, 1992.

7.   Parenthetically, we must admit there is something risible about all those *books* on paperless societies, virtual libraries, and related topics.

8.   "Kudzu, the write stuff," *Environmental Action* 25 (Winter 1994), p. 10.

all because, of course, public libraries do not replace all of their books every year. Typically, they add or replace 3 to 6 percent of their collections each year. On average, a library will circulate about 40 to 60 times as many books as it buys each year. Therefore, the true ratio is between 120 to 1 and 180 to 1—that is, electronic distribution could result in as much as *180 times* as much paper being used.

If current paper publishing is considered to be ecologically harmful, then replacing circulating public library print collections with electronic distribution and just-in-time printing would be an ecological catastrophe. It would also be an economic disaster. In most of the United States and Canada (excluding New Jersey and Massachusetts), public libraries circulated 1.6 billion books in 1991/92.[9] If we assume an average of 200 pages per book, with most adult books being longer, most children's books much shorter, and assume that color does not matter, then the cost of *printing* "just-in-time" would have been $8 billion *and* that leaves out the very high numbers of in-library and reference uses of printed materials. Remember, all these costs are just for printing—not for electronic distribution, author's royalties, editing, publishing overhead, or anything else.

Total operating budgets for those libraries for that year were just under $5 billion—$3 billion dollars short! These figures are even more disturbing when one considers that, typically, no more than 15 or 20 percent of a public library's budget goes toward materials of all kinds. So, if we put *all* the money available for public libraries into providing "just-in-time" printing we would be billions of dollars worse off *and* there would be no money for other programs or services.

---

9.   These figures and those in the preceding paragraph are derived from *American library directory 1993–94*, New Providence, N.J.: R. R. Bowker.

The Economics of Electronic Information

The fallacy of "saving trees" is small potatoes when compared to the oft-repeated assertion that everything having to do with computers is, or will shortly become, "essentially free." We are told by futurists that distribution bandwidth is essentially free, computing power is essentially free, and digital storage is essentially free.

What is the meaning of "essentially free"? Looked at objectively, it means "incredibly expensive overall, but dirt-cheap at the elemental level." For example, the Internet has been free for most people affiliated with universities, but their institutions may be writing six-figure annual checks to pay for their portion of the network and the government and its agencies have spent megabucks on creating and maintaining it. *None of this stuff is free—not now, not ever.* When futurists say technological advances mean that processing power, or communications bandwidth, or whatever, has or will become *essentially* free, they are talking nonsense. In the real world, lunches and computing have to be paid for.

Irreversible Relationships

Moore's Law says that the computer power available on a given piece of silicon (or at a given price, which is much the same thing) doubles every 18 months.[10] That has been true for microcomputers since their inception, and appears likely to be true for at least another decade. Indeed, the central processing unit (CPU) in a brand-new $3,000 computer is probably at least 64 times as powerful as the CPU in a $3,000 computer purchased nine years ago. For that matter, the new $3,000 computer will probably have about 64 times as much storage—although

---

10. The observation is attributed to Gordon E. Moore, cofounder of Intel Corporation. "Moore's Law says that the number of transistors that can be built in a given area of silicon doubles every eighteen months, which means that a new generation of faster computer hardware appears every eighteen months too." Robert X. Cringeley, *Accidental empires*, New York: HarperBusiness, 1993, p. 144.

its screen will not be 64 times as large and will not have 64 times the resolution.

Alas, the reverse is not true—that is, one cannot buy a computer today for $47 that is as useful as the $3,000 computer was nine years ago—for at least three reasons:

♦ No manufacturer or dealer can survive by selling $47 computers, particularly given that today's consumers expect some level of support. Indeed, $1,000 seems to be about the lowest viable price for a complete computer system if a minimal level of support and construction quality is to be achieved.

♦ While the $640 CPU of nine years ago may indeed still be produced and would sell for much less than $10 these days, other components of a computer system have not gone down in price as steeply. Thus, today's $500 disk drive has 50 times the capacity (and 10 times the speed) of the $500 disk drive of eight years ago—but computer manufacturers do not produce $10 disk drives today.

♦ The nine-year-old computer is nearly worthless today. Current programs will not run on it or fit on the disk drive.

Computing power continues to expand at a given price—the consumer gets more for the same price—but there is a minimum below which that price is unlikely to fall. In fact, most corporations spend far more on computing these days than in years past, if only because computer power is useless without human understanding and interpretation. The cost of human resources, of course, increases steadily.

Optical fiber provides extremely wideband communication capabilities—but that does not make communications free. This is especially true because the industries that cater to the couch-potato market continue to chew up bandwidth at a remarkable rate. It can reasonably be predicted that the cost of optical fiber and computing, and indeed the actual price of telecommunications and computing, will not be the major cost of electronic distribution of intellectual materials. Why should it be? Typesetting, printing, and distribution are not the major cost components of print publishing today. They are *significant* costs—and the costs of *maintaining* telecommunications networks, *organizing* and archiving information, and otherwise making the I-way workable will continue to be significant.

Life-Cycle Economics

Two problems occur when comparing electronic distribution to traditional print publishing. First, and already discussed, is the problem of comparing unburdened cost to fully-burdened price—that is, comparing the low incremental cost of sending a package of data over electronic networks or pressing an additional CD-ROM with the much higher final price charged for a book. Second, and to a certain extent related, is the failure to include all economic aspects of electronic distribution.

Life-cycle economic analysis or holistic economics attempts to consider the direct and indirect impact of each decision. Full life-cycle analysis is extremely difficult and complex, but the basic principle must be kept in mind when evaluating electronic distribution.[11] Deliberate exclusion of secondary costs is at the heart of many claims of the cost-effectiveness of electronic distribution. Specifically, most advocates of the all-electronic future will not allow the cost of printing individual copies by or for the end-user to be considered as part of the cost of electronic distribution. There are three arguments for this exclusion:

♦ Enlightened readers already prefer to read from the screen and rapid improvements in display technology will eliminate any remaining disadvantages to such reading.

♦ The decision to print something is an individual decision, and thus not something to be considered as part of overall economics.

---

11. Life-cycle analysis is becoming an important tool in many areas, including ecology. For example, life-cycle analysis demonstrates that, if a parent wishes to be as ecologically responsible as possible in diapering children, the choice between washable and disposable diapers will depend on where the family lives—in chronically arid areas, disposable diapers may be ecologically and economically preferable.

♦ Individual printing represents distributed costs, not really part of the cost of publication (or, for libraries, the cost of operation).

We addressed the first argument in Chapter 2. The second and third arguments deliberately warp economic comparisons and, in the third case, would represent an important philosophical shift for libraries. In practice, if most library users want printed copy, then the cost of printing *must* be considered part of the cost of electronic distribution.

Consider, for example, Lewis Carroll's two *Alice* books, readily available both as pure ASCII through electronic distribution or as inexpensive mass-market paperbacks—typeset and with illustrations. Assume $0.025 per page for individual printing (the typical cost of discounted laser supplies and copy paper; ink jet costs will be slightly higher), and assume that the electronic version can be printed out as compactly as the typeset version. The combination of these two very short books, without their illustrations, will cost $6.50 to print.[12] Therefore, we must add $6.50 to any other costs of electronic distribution to arrive at a cost basis to compare with a paperback edition.

It cannot be denied that the printed edition is more compact (printed on both sides of 6-by-9-inch paper); is more attractive and readable (including Tenniel or other illustrations and typeset for easier reading); and is the product of a viable industry. If borrowed from a library, the print edition will represent no more than $2 to $3 in overall costs—clearly a bargain. (See Chapter 9.)

This particular comparison is simplified *in favor of the electronic version* because the works are long since out of copyright. Otherwise, reasonable compensation for the author and editor would be part of both comparisons and the freely-available electronic version would not (in the long run) be free. Note that the analysis is also highly simplified; for the electronic version, it leaves out the cost of individual computers, time required to download, cost of buying and maintaining

---

12. The two texts take up 260 pages in *The complete works of Lewis Carroll,* Modern Library edition.

local printers, and energy and other costs. For the print version, it leaves out the cost of going to the bookstore or public library.

The third argument—on distributed costs—is pernicious when applied to libraries. It specifically abandons the traditional American principle of library service paid for by the community and free to the individual—a principle seen most clearly in public libraries but also applying to school, college, and university libraries. If, under this argument "free to the individual" equates to "if you want to be able to read it easily, you must have your own computer and printer and pay about $6.50," then the principle is lost, and it would be equally reasonable to charge library users $5 for each item they borrow. In either case, the institution's apparent costs are reduced by the simple expedient of concealing actual costs and shifting them to the user and the knowledge and information is no longer freely available to all, including the underprivileged who need it most. The free library is now only freely available to those with the money to pay.

Any reasonable comparison of print and electronic costs must take into account all factors, and must be based on providing equivalent services: that is, providing people with material they want in a form that is, at least, comparable to print-on-paper in ease of use. Once such a comparison is made, the all-electronic vision can be seen clearly—less a dream, more a nightmare.

Commercializing the I-Way

One drawback to the international marvel that is the Internet is its curious ability to cloud the minds of otherwise intelligent and educated men and women, making them believe that electronic communication is and will continue to be free. Against all reason, they continue to believe (based on misleading growth curves) that, in a few years, everyone will be on the Net and, best of all, electronic distribution will not cost anybody anything! There may be a few problems in getting everyone on the Net, but they are just matters of detail.

We hate to be curmudgeons but feel constrained to expose this as the fantasy it is. University administrators know that the Internet is not free—like university libraries, it has been maintained as a common good, without individual pricing or usage sensitivity. This is a very good thing—but, as with other apparently free goods, it can warp the understanding of real costs.

There are many obstacles to universal digital access, not the least of which is that many homes neither have nor are likely to purchase home computers, but one thing is clear—the "information infrastructure" or I-way will *not* be totally government supported and most assuredly will not be free. The Internet is becoming commercialized already (government funding pays for a very small percentage of total Internet costs) and this trend seems likely to continue. Moving from the Internet to a universal and possibly more coherent distribution system will surely involve huge amounts of private sector money—money that will be spent in the expectation of return.

This is no bad thing, except to those who stubbornly cling to the idea that capitalism is inherently evil and soon to be replaced by a more humane economic system. Ecologists are aware of the difficulties caused by the concept of "free goods." For example, people have polluted the air and water without concern because both are "free" and presumed to be inexhaustible. Electronic distribution as a free good represents a distortion of actual costs.

Electronic distribution as a publicly funded good makes sense only if it is funded end to end—that is, so that even the poorest American can both receive and send equitably, just as the poorest American can borrow books. That will never be the case. The I-way, a matrix of electronic networks, will be predominantly commercial and *fee-based*. Some fees may be subscriptions (monthly rates); some may be time-based; some may be usage-based, that is, based on bandwidth usage rather than connection hours.

Whatever the mix, we can be sure that the myth of free electronic distribution will be laid to rest. That being the case, strong libraries (national, public, school, and academic) with both print collections and ready access to digital resources are vital to maintain comprehensive knowledge and information services for all kinds and conditions of people. Absent those strong libraries, the I-way will be just another force contributing to an increasingly fractured and unstable society.

Points to Remember

- The universal workstation cannot meet the needs of literary scholars for primary records.

- The costs of digital conversion and storage make true universal conversion utterly impractical, even if copyright allowed for such conversion.

- Selective conversion and abandonment of the print record is a path leading to censorship and, eventually, totalitarianism.

- As long as people prefer to read from the printed page, electronic distribution with on-demand printing will be ecologically and economically disastrous as a replacement for circulating print collections and print publishing.

- There is no such thing as "essentially free" computing. While computing power for a given price will continue to increase rapidly, that does not make computing power free or computers nearly so.

- Cost models for electronic distribution that do not include the cost of printing each long text that is to be read are defective and a cover for the shifting of costs from the institution to the user. For libraries, this abandons the tradition of freely available common goods.

- The Internet never has been free. Future digital communication via the I-way will not be free.

- Without strong public libraries and continuing print collections, electronic distribution will cause further disadvantage to the already disadvantaged.

7

Enemies of the Library

All librarians are familiar with Friends of the Library (or some variant of that name)—support groups for public, academic, and even school libraries. They are groups of citizens and library users interested in promoting the library and its services and, increasingly, in raising money to supplement decreasing public or institutional funding. Demonstrably, a large portion of the public in most cities could be considered friends of libraries, even if they do not join the support organizations. There is much good will toward libraries of all kinds— often unfocused, often underexploited but real nevertheless.

The largely unchallenged virtual nonsense surrounding libraries that appears in the press, in magazines, and on TV and radio may be contributing to an erosion of that support. What is the concerned friend of libraries to make of seemingly authoritative pronouncements about an all-electronic future, the death of print, and virtual libraries? How can she or he be expected to put time, money, and effort into supporting institutions that pundits say are on the way out?

The people who are misleading library supporters are not enamored of spending money on library buildings, collections, services and staff, and they know all too well that more than 70 percent of academic library budgets may go to salaries and wages. They delight in the idea that a "virtual library" does not require a building or tangible collections—after all, electronic resources are free, are they not? It is a safe bet that their idea of a virtual library is one without all those salaries and wages, too.

Among the enemies of libraries are those futurists who see print as irrelevant and doomed and the technovandals who see no point in preserving the boring records of the obsolete past and present. The most fervid advocates of the death of print are enemies of libraries, either directly or because they regard libraries and librarians, when they think about them at all, as archaic and pointless. Such people really do not like books, or reading for that matter, and tend to believe that the only things that matter in any book are discrete paragraphs of information. If it is not electronic, in the simple primary-colored mental world they inhabit, it is obsolete. Jane Austen? Leo Tolstoy? Dante? Bertrand Russell? De Toqueville? Or, for that matter, Sara Paretsky, Philip José Farmer, Maya Angelou, Dave Barry? Why go to the mental strain of reading and having to create your own mental images when you can play a graphic computer game or watch television? Nobody reads anymore, say the inhabitants of the surreal world of multimedia and virtual reality. If it were true, how sad it would be, but it is not true and those who care about learning and society should know the battle is by no means lost.

The Enemies Within

Perhaps the most distressing group of enemies of libraries are those within the profession—librarians and library educators who devalue the profession and would flee from both the name and the practice of librarianship if their livelihoods did not depend on it.

Suicidal Librarians

It is profoundly discouraging to read that the head of a public library system, a person who calls himself a "chief executive" rather than a library director, has turned all the librarians into "information specialists." Every white-collar worker, professional or not, could be called an information specialist. It is a bland, meaningless term that weakens the position of the people who carry it and weakens the libraries (or should that be "information centers"?) in which they work. As many Chief Information Officers in corporations have found to their dismay, empty titles lead to short life-spans. A city's population is less likely to turn out for its branch information centers than for its branch libraries. Calling public librarians "information specialists" also suggests that the only function of public libraries is to provide information, a drastic and suicidal oversimplification.

It is encouraging to see the Librarian of Congress (who, mercifully, does not call himself the CEO of the Information Center of Congress) testifying before Congress that electronic information "will supplement, not destroy, the book," pointing out the many virtues of public libraries, and asserting that there is really no practical, user-friendly substitute for the book. He sees public libraries as serving future electronic information needs for those who cannot otherwise afford them—but in addition to, not instead of, providing books and other paper materials. The Librarian of Congress does not have an MLS. The head of the public library system alluded to does have an MLS. Which professional serves libraries better?

Doomcryers in Library Schools

Another set of disturbing anti-library, anti-librarian sentiments comes from faculty in library schools, some of whom are among the most ardent death-of-print advocates. A minority of the people who are educating future librarians appear not to believe in the future of libraries despite the fact that the majority of their students go to library school to become librarians and end up working in libraries.

It sometimes seems that the only people who believe in the myth of the "opportunities" offered in the "emerging information professions" are these anti-library educators. If they eliminate "library" from the names of their schools and turn off the students who are their livelihood, how can they be surprised when their schools are seen as marginal and, in some cases, shut down? Fortunately, some of the most effective debunking of death-of-print mythology has also come from within the library schools and it is likely that most library school faculty understand that the future requires both print and electronics.

Librarianship will die if librarians and library educators kill it off. A profession made up of people who think it is doomed and act as if it is irrelevant is not a good insurance risk. If these trends intensify, the ultimate sufferer will be the poor everyday library user.

Disintermediation

Another suicidal trend is the push for disintermediation[1]—the idea that each user should become her or his own reference librarian. Library instruction, commonly but erroneously called "bibliographic instruction," is certainly a good thing. Of course college students need to have research skills and those who have been adversely affected by the decline of the high-school library need those skills most. Certainly some people will make direct use of reference sources in the future, thus bypassing the librarian and, sometimes, the library itself.

There is little that is new about people obtaining information directly—it can be argued that the history of progress in librarianship is one of decreasing the need for mediation. What else are public catalogues, open shelves, accessible reference collections, etc., all about? After all, the ultimate mediated library is the monastic library described in *The name of the rose*[2]—one that, for all its virtues, is scarcely the *beau ideal* of a modern library!

The question therefore is not the presence or absence of mediation but the degree of mediation that is desirable and affordable. Yet extremists call for the *end* of reference librarianship and promote the idea that *every* user in *every* library should be handling all research work and coping with all research resources. There are at least two fundamental flaws in this position:

---

1.   One good rule of thumb in librarianship and elsewhere is: the uglier the neologism, the more undesirable the notion it describes. *Vide* "outsourcing."

2.   Umberto Eco, *The name of the rose*, San Diego: Harcourt Brace Jovanovich, 1985.

♦ It denies that reference librarianship is a professional activity, seeing it as no more skilled than driving a car or reading a map. Such thinking devalues one of librarianship's most valuable aspects, and in so doing equates professional librarians with clerks. This would be bad enough if it were coming from the outside; it is self-destructive coming from within librarianship.

♦ It assumes that ordinary library users have some reason to build and maintain research skills that are strong enough to eliminate the need for reference librarians. Why should they? For most people, detailed reference work is not an everyday act. Even assuming that most adults *could* learn to do most of their own car repair, plumbing, and electrical work—an assumption leading to an even more dangerous world than today's—why on earth would they?

A casual reading of the introductory matter of almost any scholarly work will yield effusive thanks from the scholar-author for the invaluable help (a.k.a. mediation) of many reference librarians. This is one of the great selling points of librarianship. It makes no sense to throw it away in the name of "disintermediation."

It would be astonishing to hear of plumbers or electricians giving speeches in favor of disintermediation—that is, the desirability of training everybody to do his or her own plumbing or electrical work. Even law firms that provide paralegal services are careful to emphasize the value of trained lawyers—not a lot of disintermediation there. Is reference librarianship so much less specialized and valuable than plumbing and electrical work? Why do some librarians but no lawyers wish their profession out of existence?

Given the continuing theme of disintermediation in the library field, it is hardly surprising to read of a well-known UC Berkeley anthropology professor asserting that the Anthropology Library absolutely needed to remain—but that the department could run it with student assistants and get rid of the reference librarians! If librarians do not value reference librarianship as a professional activity, why should professors?

Which current and future new computer tools will make librarians obsolete? Futurists hand-wave about automatic indexing, deep syntactical analysis leading to multilevel user-guided structures, and so on. Do any of these work in the real world? If they do, none has been demonstrated to do so outside minute, specialized, and hand-picked realms. We have already seen that using WAIS rather than traditional online catalogue methods to control even a small collection leads to much more difficulty in retrieving desired items. The futurists predict, however, that new tools will take the place of reference librarians, no matter what the cost in the devaluation of retrieval. This could be one prediction of the futurists that may happen. If it does it will be because the tools are used in place of reference librarians for want of anything better and because librarians themselves have devalued their role enough for those outside to believe that a computer can do as well. Lemmings have exhibited superior survival instincts.

Abandoning the Commons

Foolish ideas are often encapsulated in slick tags. "Access not ownership" was a popular line in the bumpersticker school of library thought until it occurred to someone that if nobody owned anything, there would be nothing to which to gain access. "Just in time not just in case" (referring to library materials) is the latest slogan. It does for collection development what disintermediation does for reference service.

The idea is that even the largest university libraries should acquire items only when they are currently in demand. Some learned colleagues take that idea one step further—get rid of all the journal subscriptions and centralized collections and just send books and articles directly to scholars when they are needed. This, not surprisingly, has been embraced enthusiastically by bureaucrats and technovandals.[3] When will we stop engaging in the intellectual equivalent of giving aid and comfort (not to mention ammunition) to the enemy? The economic

---

3. Michael Gorman, "The treason of the learned," *Library Journal* 119 (February 15, 1994), pp. 130–131.

implications of the trend away from collections are discussed in Chapter 8, but something needs to be said here about the social issue.

The elimination of collection development and maintenance, the elimination of a tangible public access collection, amounts to no less than abandoning the commons. We recognize that most institutions cannot maintain wholly comprehensive collections—and have never been able to, for that matter—but we feel the line should be drawn long before the common pool of historical and current material is abandoned altogether. All arts and humanities fields require access to rich collections that cut across many disciplines, as do most social science disciplines and *all* new fields of study. Just-in-time will not cut it. Scholars and students in almost all fields need background, history, interdisciplinary material, and browsing. This is true of scientists and some technologists, but they tend to be less aware of the need.

We will set aside the fact that "just-in-time" policies should be called "available-at-some-time" policies because "just-in-time" is, ironically, only truly achievable by direct access to real collections. Just-in-time policies, as a general replacement for sound collection development, are suicidal.

The New Barbarians

"Now what I want is Facts—Facts alone are important in life."[4] To a new barbarian, a book is just a chance aggregation of independent paragraphs that would inherently be more usable and valuable were they freed from their linear arrangement and made accessible separately. The new barbarians denigrate prose, philosophy, history and fiction by equating it with cheap genre fiction. Facts are all-important—and a current fact is the highest achievement of humankind.

The new barbarians speak confidently of the time it takes for a book or article to become obsolete, by which they mean worthless. They use percentages and statistics to determine that

---

4.   The words of Thomas Gradgrind in Charles Dickens' *Hard times*, book 1, chapter 1.

time, which is usually quite short. This rapid obsolescence eliminates the problem of massive conversion, since old books and articles have nothing worthwhile to offer in any case. For the new barbarians, there are no exceptions. Old is bad, new is good, and everything is better when done electronically.

The new barbarians want personalized electronic daily newspapers, to feed the solipsism that is central to their contextless lives. The new barbarians simplify every field they touch. That which can be done partially by computer should be done entirely by computer. That which cannot be done by computer either will be done by computer in the future or is not worth doing anyway. The people who provide the services that computers will take over are redundant and should find something else to do.

When the business equivalents of new barbarians function in top corporate management, they tend to become very rich—and their companies get much smaller, leaving thousands out on the streets while impoverishing the richness of the society. That, naturally, is not their problem.

The new barbarians are at the gate. They will *prove* that the all-electronic virtual library is cheaper and better than boring old print or some confused combination of print and electronic. They are already "proving" to some university management teams that the road to vibrant health for the university is to eliminate everything that does not return top dollar to graduates; in other words, they are turning universities into vocational schools.

For libraries, the situation is even simpler. A vocational school does not need millions of books; mostly, it needs the electronic equivalent of a good bookstore. It certainly does not need all those librarians and library workers, and that goes for all those students earning their way through college on work-study and other jobs. If all the workers are fired, the virtual library becomes cheaper than a real library—and ever so much better, since all it will offer is up-to-date facts in the handful of areas that contribute to the profitability of University, Inc.

The new barbarians want to destroy library buildings and library jobs. Recently, a senior university administrator told a conference he thought there would never be a need for new or expanded library buildings since the existing buildings would most likely be empty in a decade. When it comes to jobs, remember that the only economic models that offer plausible savings through all-electronic libraries do so by the expedient of eliminating the majority of academic library costs—salaries and hourly wages.

The new barbarism is not exclusive to academia. There are those who view public libraries staffed with librarians and offering print materials as a complete waste of time and money. In their view, what we need are sitting rooms in each neighborhood staffed by volunteers offering a handful of best-sellers and tips on how to use home infotainment centers to obtain the up-to-date facts that are all a modern person really needs. More, what do school children need with school libraries? Surely their home computers and VCRs will give them everything that the few textbooks cannot supply. Hard Times indeed when the dreams of children are to be fed by facts and shallow images because, in a mean-spirited world, that is all we can afford to give them.

The new barbarism has found its new barbaric yawp.[5] John Kountz set out the new agenda in a remarkable article published in 1992.[6] The piece exhibits all the attributes of the new barbarian in the purest, most complete form. He begins with an unsubstantiated assumption—"In the next five years or so, the market for—and the availability of—information printed on paper can be anticipated to shrink by 50 per cent. By the turn of the century, paper will satisfy less than 5 per cent of the total commerce in information." As we write, two and a half years into the "next five years or so," this remarkable shrinkage has not yet begun.

Kountz goes on to warn librarians that they are in danger of becoming "curators of an archaic intellectual delivery system for paper artifacts" unless they get with the paperless program. Not to worry though, there is a solution: another dream toy—

5.　"I sound my barbaric yawp over the roofs of the world." Walt Whitman, *Song of myself*, 51.

6.　John Kountz, "Tomorrow's libraries: more than a modular telephone jack, less than a complete revolution—perspectives of a provocateur," *Library Hi Tech* 10, no. 4 (1992), pp. 39–50.

this time the "tablet computer." Not that the device has actually been developed or demonstrated yet, but it will be any day now.

In case there is any doubt, we are informed that "[e]ventually some kind of information appliance (computer) designed to facilitate the delivery and use of information will replace traditional library service for almost all subject disciplines." There follow some references to an impressive sounding list of gadgets and capabilities that will culminate in a device stated, rather precisely, to have "a unit price of about $300.00." By the year 2000, indeed, "like the quartz wristwatch or the ball point pen, what began as a costly luxury will be an inexpensive, mass-market commodity."

This article contains much about the cost of libraries (but says nothing of their value); the inevitability of migration to electronics; and the need for the library as reading room with "teaser" materials (whatever the latter may be). There is a lot about information, especially as a commodity, but nothing about knowledge, nothing about civilization, nothing about education, nothing about learning.

The world of the new barbarian is bleak indeed. Its mechanistic antivision must be countered forcefully in an affirmative, humanistic fashion if we are to have thriving libraries.

Points to Remember

📖 Libraries should recognize and encourage their friends while being aware of their enemies.

📖 Librarians do important work. Changing the name of the profession cheapens and threatens its future.

📖 Scholars appreciate reference librarians, and so should other librarians. The push for universal disintermediation is suicidal.

📖 A good library is not a subsidized bookstore, and librarians are not stock clerks.

8

The Diversity of Libraries

Despite their commonalities of mission and interest, libraries are diverse. Large libraries differ from small libraries; urban libraries from small town or rural; publicly funded from privately funded. The essence of each library is defined by the community it serves. The needs and problems of academic libraries and their patrons are not necessarily the needs and problems of public or school libraries. These differences, though real, should not be exaggerated.

Public libraries are not primarily research institutions, but research does take place in even comparatively small public libraries; moreover, several major urban public libraries are, quite appropriately, members of the Association of Research Libraries. University libraries do not exist to provide for leisure needs—but every good university library has collections of fiction, videos, sound recordings, etc., that are used for research, teaching, *and* entertainment. What unites libraries is more important than the distinctions between libraries—it is imperative that libraries should cooperate for mutual benefit.

Even within types of library, one can see differences. For example, the needs and problems of major university libraries are not those of all university libraries and the university library is a different entity from the college library. Even within the ranks of major university libraries, problems and possible solutions vary enormously. Moreover, part of a large diffuse university library is by no means the whole—the problems, pressures, and needs of a physical sciences library are very different from those of a social science or humanities service. Libraries have much in common; libraries differ one from the other; and the work and mission of a librarian is largely defined by the milieu within which she or he works. These statements are not mutually exclusive. Libraries are a complex subset of a complex world and it behooves librarians and those interested in libraries to understand that complexity.

Simple Answers to Complex Questions

He who accounts all things easy will have many difficulties.
Lao Tse

Many people do not deal with complexity very well. They want simple paths to be navigated with simple instructions. Even when they understand that change is necessary, they want that change spelled out in simple terms, so they can make the big jump and never think about the issue again. This mind-set bedevils the body politic—half the ills of the modern world would be cured if only citizens would accept that complex problems may have only complex solutions at best and that some problems may never be resolved completely.

The Danger of Oversimplification

We inhabit a complex world. There is no evidence whatsoever that it will grow less complex—that would require the reversal of every historic trend. Complexity, however, is uncomfortable; it bothers lots of people. This is especially true of the kind of complexity that demands constant change. Some librarians want to jump from the old definition of librarianship to a wonderful, if fuzzy, and wholly new definition—then stop thinking about it again. This simplistic view of change in libraries is not confined to the United States. Witness this statement from Singapore:

> The librarian of the future will no longer be a custodian of dusty books on the shelves but a computer whiz who will sort and sell information, now choking a borderless world.[1]

Such a simple, one-time redefinition is impossible. The only reasonable paradigm for librarianship involves constant change and continuing redefinition. This applies to all library activities and services: to the balance between collection development and remote access; to the acquisition and cataloguing of knowledge and information in all media; to the role of the reference librarian; to the content and delivery of library instruction programs; and on and on.

We might be falling into the mind-set that we have excoriated in saying that simple answers are *always* wrong answers. Simple answers can be found for simple problems but few complex problems have realistic simple answers. Let us say that, in the real world, simple solutions generally reduce understanding of a situation to the point that they are rarely useful.

Librarians have been warned that, if they refuse to board the death-of-print bandwagon, they will see a future in which libraries will not be the means by which most people obtain the information they need. This is supposed to come as a "shock! horror!" revelation, but the truth is that libraries have *never* been the sole, or even the primary, source of information for the majority of people. Good libraries serve many important purposes, but they never have been universal sources, and they never will be. To reduce this argument to the absurdity it is, we are being told that libraries are obsolete because they can no longer be something that they never have been or wished to be!

1.　N. Nirmala, "Master plan puts the byte on librarians: computer links will turn them into information brokers," *Straits Times Weekly Edition*, March 26, 1994.

"The Future," "The Library," and "The Patron"

In many ways, "The Library" is an absurdly simplistic formulation, as is "The Patron." The corporate library for a genetic engineering company has different needs, and serves very different patrons, from a good neighborhood branch of a public library. The University of California, Berkeley, Physics Library has a very different role from the UCB Doe Main Library with its massive collections in the humanities and social sciences, and should allocate its funds differently. So should the library of a community college, which, again, serves very different needs and very different patrons.

A single solution to future information needs may make sense for some specialized libraries. Such libraries are rare—far rarer than most futurists will admit. These are libraries with patrons who value only current data or information. These are libraries whose patrons think of reading solely as a way to update their own internal databases. Finally, these are libraries serving subject areas in which virtually all information is electronic or soon will be.

Most libraries—even very specialized libraries—serve patrons with much more complex needs and, therefore, must adopt more diversified approaches to the future. One solution will not fit all, and adopting the simple "electronics-only" solution will endanger the libraries and librarians who do so. If a library's sole solution is electronic, that library will remove itself from the past and from the world of knowledge. That is as absurd as a library confining itself solely to print and other non-electronic sources, thus removing itself from the world of current, accessible data and information. The truth lies in a mix—a mix that will vary from library to library but only in the rarest instances will involve complete dominance by any one medium of communication.

Libraries: Not Just Facts

Thinking librarians know full well that libraries are much more than just repositories of data and information. The latter is an important function of libraries but it certainly is not everything.

Libraries are places to learn—places in which to become knowledgeable. They also provide entertainment, serendipity, the opportunity to find out about a host of practical matters, and all the treasures of the human mind. For children, school and public libraries are places in which they can become interested in reading and embark on the life-long process of increasing literacy. They are also places for children to delight in the whole range of human communication and to understand the power of the image as well as the word. Libraries are social places—centers of their communities, campuses, and institutions. These are all appropriate roles.[2]

Libraries serve many purposes. Some library functions can be carried out better through electronic means, either within the library or outside. Other library functions cannot fit neatly into computer-based systems. Librarians need to be aware of everything they do, need to value each of the services they provide to their patrons, and need to make their funding agencies aware of their services—their diversity and strengths.

Librarians also need to be aware—as most good public librarians already are—that many libraries serve economically disadvantaged patrons, particularly those temporarily out of work or stuck in a cycle of semi-employment, in ways unequaled by other agencies. For such libraries to put all their resources into electronics would be to abandon those patrons, who cannot afford the fees for computer access and are unlikely to have their own computers. Without vibrant, freely available public libraries and libraries of public institutions, they will be even more disadvantaged. Publicly supported libraries are remarkable, multi-faceted institutions. Society needs them to prosper, and cannot allow them to be swamped by the fads of single-minded futurism.

The Need for Balance

There is a great discontinuity in the working lives of librarians of all kinds today. On the one hand, there are the omnipresent

---

2.   The particular roles and strengths of public libraries are discussed in more detail in Chapter 9.

pressures of staffing services, maintaining libraries and their services, simply making sure that materials are acquired, catalogued, checked out, and checked in—in short, the common task, the daily round that makes a library *work*. On the other hand, there are futuristic dreams and nightmares—the feeling that somehow, some time soon, everything will be changed utterly. Small wonder that so many librarians want to give up on the daily grind and trust in, or fear, the electronic Wizard of Oz. If the Wiz is going to be the salvation or doom of libraries, why worry about today?

Alas, as with the Wizard, there is less there than meets the eye. The true prescription for successful libraries lies in boring old moderation and balance. There *is* a yellow brick road but it leads to neither heaven nor hell—it leads to future libraries that will use appropriate technology appropriately and preserve and make available all forms of human communication. To achieve progress through balance, librarians *should* read and analyze the arguments for revolutionary change; but they should temper that reading with the understanding that almost all change is evolutionary.

Immediate Access to Appropriate Resources

Library users expect libraries to have a variety of resources and to serve a variety of needs. There is a need for data and information, but there is also a need for knowledge, literature, entertainment, and all else that nourishes the mind. Library users value materials that they can have immediately over those that may arrive later—that has been demonstrated time and time again. The preference is not at all unreasonable and is understandable to all but the most mechanistic of librarians. Currency and definitiveness are important attributes, but they pale beside ease of use and availability. That tends to be true even for scholarly library users; after all, an essential precondition of scholarship is setting aside seemingly relevant materials that are, in fact, not germane—something that is only feasible on a large scale with direct access.

Library users want resources delivered in a manner that suits their needs and wishes. When it comes to data and information, that convenient delivery is increasingly accomplished by electronic means. When it comes to knowledge and entertainment, for the indefinite future, access will mean books, videos, records, etc., that are available for use—*even if* the available material is not the most current and *even if* the content is available online. This may seem a disgracefully backward state of affairs to the futurists, but who is to say that the mass of library users are wrong because they do not have or desire ready access to terminals, are unwilling to pay communications charges, simply profer print-on-paper, and have a human preference for what they can understand and use most readily? In the words of Sandra Ballasch:

> It is well to remember that sometimes the user of an item (physical or not) really does know what suits him or her best. It may be wise not to assume that we experts always know just how people will respond to the changes we propose for their benefit . . . The object is always to get to the user what they want in a form they can afford and can use. If we go so far as to provide information (for want of a better word) in forms and at places no one wants, what have we accomplished—for them, for us and for the larger community?[3]

To Serve and Preserve

Librarians need always to remember the enduring mission of libraries. Different people state that mission in different ways, but here is a concise version that we believe to be useful:

> Libraries and librarians serve their users and preserve the culture by acquiring, listing, making available, and conserving the records of humankind in all media and by providing services to the users of those records.

A library must know who its current and potential users are and must know their needs. The groups will be different, obviously, for different libraries. A library serves those users by providing them with recorded data, information, and knowl-

---

3.   Electronic message on PACS-L, March 17, 1994.

edge for enlightenment and entertainment in ways that the users and librarians agree fall within the individual mission of an individual library. That never means that any one library can possibly serve *all* the information, enlightenment, and entertainment needs of its users; none ever has and none ever will. It does mean that each library has its own mix of services and mix of means of communication.

A university physics library that spends more on books than on journals and that has no plans to transfer a significant part of its materials budget to electronic and other new media is a physics library in serious trouble. A neighborhood public library that spends much more on books than on magazines, almost nothing on journals, and is not planning to invest heavily in electronic access and new media is probably serving its community well. Different strokes for different libraries and library users. These are examples of libraries at opposite ends of the electronic / print range; most libraries fall somewhere in the middle.

Some libraries have, among their primary missions, that of preserving the record of the culture. No institution other than the library carries out this mission as well. Although preservation is one of the missions of libraries, it is not the mission of every library. It should be remembered, however, that each library has a part in preservation, however small, because each library has an element of singularity. The role of each library in passing on the culture will differ.

Every branch public library should have the works of William Shakespeare, a reasonable collection of other classic literature, some classic movies on video, and some sound recordings of, for example, Beethoven, even though those materials will not circulate as often as genre novels, how-to books, and popular videos and CDs. Cultural artifacts—not only the best books, films, and recordings, but also currently popular books, magazines, and other materials—need to be available in enough locations, and cared for well enough, that future historians and users can see how our culture has evolved. Electronic media, particularly CD-ROM and laserdisc, have enormous potential in this area, making it feasible for even smaller libraries to provide access to the raw materials of the culture.

To take but one example, the Library of Congress's American Memory Project[4] is an important use of multimedia technology to expand services and enrich our cultural memory by allowing searching and display of LC's archival collections (text, graphics, audio, and video). Unlike some of the fevered dreams of the futurists, the American Memory Project does not threaten existing collections and services—it expands upon them. It is a boon to libraries, not a harbinger of their death. These are materials of great interest but not such that the average user needs to have them available at home or will wish to download them—but what a wonderful thing to have available at the neighborhood library when needed! The availability of such resources cannot be an excuse for doing away with the original artifacts because there are many cases in which only the artifact will do.

Celebrating Diversity and Complexity

Librarians should value and celebrate the complexity and diversity of the records of humankind. There is really nothing new about diversity of library collections. It is hard to conceive of a public library collection in 1993 (or 1963, for that matter) containing nothing but printed hardcover books. Even major research libraries have incorporated sound recordings, films, etc. (not to mention the "other" print resources—maps, scores, etc.) into their still primarily book-based collections. Books are themselves very diverse, encompassing as they do all human experience and thought. Even so, it has been many moons since most libraries relied solely on books.

Diversity is *inherently* a good thing, which makes it curious that some futurists disdain it so. Any thoughtful observer will agree that electronic distribution of data and information will be used more in the future than it was in the past. Why proceed from that to *narrow* the choices of means of communication by suggesting that books and other non-electronic forms will or should cease to be published and used? Such a stance is

---

4.   Jean Armour Polly and Elaine Lyon, "Out of the archives and into the streets: American memory in American libraries," *Online* 16 (September 1992), pp. 51–56.

ignorant and ahistorical. It limits rather than expands and imposes uniformity rather than encouraging creative diversity.

Indeed, diversity within electronic distribution is a far more exciting prospect than the idea that the user will be enslaved to one big network supplying all of her or his needs. CD-ROM and other digital publications are useful tools in the diverse ways that libraries serve their patrons. So are microfiche and microfilm (for all their many limitations); so are videocassettes, videodiscs, compact discs, print magazines, and books. So are online searches of national bibliographic databases, of commercial databases, and of Internet resources. We have been promised (or threatened with) a single, shiny, immortal, electronic bloom when human history prefigures and the human mind demands a communications garden of a thousand different and differently colored flowers.

The Future of Libraries: Paradigms and Projections

Library conferences and library journals are abuzz with talk of paradigm shifts . . . the non-library . . . the library without walls . . . the library as electronic switching center . . . and on and on. Meanwhile, most librarians get on with the essential daily tasks involved in incorporating new technologies into existing services; maintaining and improving existing collections; and generally making real if unspectacular progress in the face of financial adversity. Some futurists are convinced that library users want only hot electronic information; either libraries change to meet their needs, or libraries become obsolete. This presupposes rather a lot about the library user and is a profoundly elitist and negative view.

There has always been a gap between what goes on in library school classes and what goes on in libraries, but that is minuscule compared with the gap between the realities of library life and the dreams of some futurists. The absolute predictions of the latter are made in the comfortable knowledge that nobody will denounce them, or even remember, when those projections do not come true. The smart thing is to make projections for decades in the future; with luck, the prophet will be dead before the projections turn out to be wrong.

We see a future in which libraries *as we know them* will be central to society for decades to come. By libraries as we know them we mean libraries with the same enduring commitments and the same desire to incorporate new technologies while preserving what is good of the old. A century from now? That is harder to say—for one thing, it assumes that there will be civilization a century from now. On the other hand, the world of 1994 is completely different from the world of 1894, yet libraries have, *in essence*, changed far less than most other institutions. Then as now, innovation was important to libraries, as were literacy, learning, and service. It is not at all implausible that, in the unimaginable world of 2094, the library might be recognizable to a library user of today.

Projecting from False Pasts

One problem with futurism is that future library needs are often based on false pasts and misperceptions of the present. Let us look at two yesterdays that never were and an implausible future based on a false present.

"When Libraries Were the Primary Sources for Up-to-Date Information"

It is alleged that, if libraries do not take drastic action, they will no longer be the primary sources for the most up-to-date information. As a consequence, people will bypass libraries for other, more current, sources. This would be a dire prediction were it not based on a bogus premise.

Just when has the library ever been the key source for the most up-to-the-minute information? How many people call their public libraries to check on traffic conditions? What percentage of daily newspaper reading takes place at the public library? Have business people trying to keep up with an industry ever relied on the public library for the latest information—or have they subscribed to the industry weeklies, specialized newsletters, and, lately, online services?

Most people, particularly most people outside academia, use the library to fill in the pieces, to provide resources that they do not need every day. That is typical behavior whenever everyday resources are reasonably priced. No serious investor would rely on a library as the only source of investment information—but those considering some new investments or evaluating mutual funds may very well use public libraries as their starting point. A physicist will not count on a library to keep up with her primary area of interest, but a student or humanist will go to the library to gain basic understanding of an unfamiliar area.

In the context of information, libraries generally deal more in information that someone has organized with some thought than in late-breaking news and raw data. That has always been their primary role and should continue to be. It is not the most glamorous role, but it is important and realistic. More to the point, it is a role that libraries can do well. To abandon that role in order to shift all resources into the provision of up-to-the-minute electronic data is a hopeless quest for centrality for the privileged few.

People will not abandon their other means of acquiring the current information that they need (or want) the most. There is no good reason for them to suddenly turn to the library for what they can do better on their own. On the other hand, those who rely on the library for the cultural record and for useful, if less absolutely current, material on subjects of secondary interest, will be disappointed and will turn against the library.

There is no evidence to suggest that libraries can succeed in what is fundamentally a nontraditional role and it would be suicidal to abandon the traditional role that has made libraries central to campuses and important to communities in an attempt to do so. That new role is, in any case, one that works well only within the scientific, technical and medical spheres of academic and special libraries. A public library or a library of a liberal arts college or community college would betray its users and destroy itself in the process by focusing on an all-electronic, up-to-the-minute future.

"When Everyone Was Literate, and All Adults Were Book Buyers"

Some futurists (no-futurists, in this case) say that libraries should abandon books for virtual reality and multimedia, because we have left the era in which everyone was literate and all adults purchased and read books. No one would dispute that literacy is a problem. When was this not so? Ah yes, those wonderful decades when every adult American read books as a primary means of leisure—and when they all had the leisure to read books. Can anyone place those decades in history? Back before book and magazine publishing began their dramatic decline? Back when every American took the daily newspaper? Just when were those decades, and why did they end?

Those times never existed and total book and magazine publishing has not declined. There is a natural tendency to romanticize the past, to imagine it as an animated Norman Rockwell painting. Why, Abraham Lincoln, a typical nine-teenth century kind of guy, was so desperate to read that he did it by the light of the fireplace. Maybe so, but how many others did the same? What was the adult literacy rate in Lincoln's time? The remarkable thing is that, today, two-thirds of American adults use their public libraries—and most studies show that public library use is increasing, in some cases dramatically.

Modern Americans read. They may not all be buying books (though the growth of book superstores does not suggest a dying marketplace), but there has never been a period when everyone read books. As with universal literacy, universal book reading is a wonderful goal and one toward which we should work but is not a description of any period of American history.

One big difference between now and then is that we can no longer pretend that the rest of the population is somehow subhuman or ignore their very existence. It is also true that nonreaders have increasingly serious handicaps in today's and tomorrow's society. *The only way to have an equitable society is to have universal literacy.* It is a cop-out to say "Well, nobody reads any more, so we will do away with books." The true course is for libraries to be involved in adult literacy work; to keep and expand children's book-reading programs; and to keep on keeping on in the face of false nostalgia and futuristic blather. When children are taught to love books, they grow up to be readers. When adults dismiss books as irrelevant, their children are less likely to be readers—and they will live with the consequences all the rest of their lives.

"When Most Information Is Electronic, Public Libraries Will Be Obsolete"

Perhaps the most disheartening ploy in the futurist's routine is the simple assertion that most information will be electronic in the future, with direct access by the user, thus making public libraries obsolete. Let us grant that they mean information rather than data—that is, processed data having some useful meaning to people. Most is not all, and that is an important distinction. Saying that most information will be electronic is, in and of itself, essentially meaningless for libraries, particularly for public libraries. So what? The average public library does not acquire most published books, and it does not subscribe to most journals (indeed, it probably subscribes to a tiny percentage of journals, as opposed to magazines). Does that make the public library worthless? Not according to the two-thirds of American adults who use public libraries; even those who are seeking information (and not knowledge and entertainment) cannot use all the information the library has.

"The MTV Generation" and the Printed Word

Futurists say that libraries must abandon the printed word because young people today—the MTV Generation—have abandoned the printed word. They assert that print literacy is dying out, and that future generations will not possess the attention span needed to read books and magazines. The clear lesson of this statement is that libraries should be stocking up on videos and saving money for virtual reality systems.

Quite apart from the shallowness and banality of stereotyping entire generations based on the excesses of some, these assertions are both untrue and dangerous even if based on a thread of reality. Illiteracy and aliteracy—knowing how to read, but not reading—are serious social problems with which libraries should be directly concerned.

The portion of society that does not read, that cannot or will not deal with coherent linear text, is the portion of society doomed to being an underclass—subject to manipulation and exploitation thanks to that unwillingness and short attention span. Libraries and librarians should be part of the effort to *overcome* aliteracy and illiteracy, not willing accomplices in the educational disenfranchisement of a generation. Libraries cannot do the right thing by devoting their resources to electronic information—which primarily serves the elite—or by substituting entertainment videos for books.

This is not to suggest that libraries should stay away from videocassettes, sound recordings, or even virtual reality packages if that technology ever makes sense for the library market, any more than they should avoid mystery, science fiction, or romance novels. Libraries are about entertainment *as well as* enlightenment—but in balance. Libraries are about empowering the unempowered through knowledge and information—not about participating in the distribution of an electronic opiate of the people.

Elitism and Irrelevance: The Greatest Dangers

The provision of networked information is now predominantly a service to the elite—a large elite, to be sure, but an elite nonetheless. Telling average public library patrons or average undergraduate students that they can traverse the Web to find a good WAIS server that may help them locate the information they really need is basically telling them to go to hell. Right now, there's nothing in the development of the I-way that suggests elitism will cease to be a factor in online electronic access—or, despite some hand-waving, that the elite seriously want that elitism to end.

Access to the Internet is nontrivial even for those who have the money and connections. It demands a level of computer literacy and interest far beyond what the average person has *or needs* in her or his daily life. Even if 20 million Americans have access to the Internet or interconnected networks, as vaguely supported as that estimate is, that means that more than 200 million Americans *do not* have such access. Tens of millions of Americans may have no need for, or interest in, such access but most of them do use libraries and do read books.

Perhaps the most bizarre aspect of the new elitism, the push for virtual libraries, is that it is a case of telling the populace what they should need, even though it is not what they want. As noted in the Research Libraries Group report *Preferred Futures for Libraries*:

> When push comes to shove, faculty want materials on campus. They don't want to be dependent on other distant libraries for needed materials. Many of them also, because of the structure of their disciplines, still depend on at-the-shelf browsing. Efforts by librarians to de-emphasize ownership are interpreted as a failure to understand both the political environment and legitimate differences in research methodologies among disciplines.[5]

Some of us, apparently, know better. Or do we? As Steven Kirby (University of Georgia) says:

> Faculty and advanced graduate students at research universities are the most likely beneficiaries of the virtual library. This is the group that most often makes use of obscure, possibly expensive, and seldom used materials. And if the prime beneficiaries have reservations about the benefits of the virtual library, then who are we building it for?[6]

Perhaps, as some have noted, because it may be possible to do so—and because some librarians have lost sight of the ends of librarianship; their eyes blinded by their fascination with the means. A library (virtual or real) that addresses neither the needs *nor the preferences* of its users is an irrelevant library— one that will become *truly* virtual, since it will lose its funding and cease to exist.

---

5.   Richard M. Dougherty and Carol Hughes, *Preferred futures for libraries: a summary of six workshops with university provosts and library directors*, Mountain View, Calif.: Research Libraries Group, 1991, p. 6.

6.   Electronic communication on PACS-L, March 3, 1992.

Points to Remember

📖 There is no such thing as "The Library" or "The Patron." Different libraries and different library users have different needs and problems.

📖 Simple solutions assume simple futures, but every realistic indication is that the future will be more complex than the present.

📖 Libraries are not just storehouses of data and information. Pure fact-seeking represents a minority use of libraries.

📖 Library users tend to know what they want and prefer, and librarians would do well to pay attention to those wants and preferences.

📖 Most library users want resources that they can use and that are immediately available, even if they are not necessarily the newest resources.

📖 Memories of the past tend to be defectively rosy. Libraries have never been the sole sources or best sources of up-to-date information and there has never been a society in which everyone read books.

📖 Librarians and libraries must beware shifting their resources to serve only the computer-literate elite. They must also be wary of telling their users what they need when it is not what they want. Either course risks irrelevance and doom.

9

Economics of Collection
and Access

There are those who believe that library service should be
based entirely on access on demand. They believe that,
as a consequence, libraries should abandon collection
development (and, ultimately, abandon the collection altogether). With "access" (a code word for the virtual library) as
the dominant policy, a library will obtain or give access to the
texts and graphics their users request *at the time of the request*—
by borrowing hard copy from somewhere else, printing from an
electronic database, or directing the user to a terminal that gives
access to relevant databases. It should be noted that the borrowing of hard copy is seen by these futurists as an interim and
soon-to-be obsolete measure. The battle lines are drawn—access is good, collections are bad, and they are, eventually,
mutually exclusive.

This is an extreme statement of a likely future—one that is
so distorted as to be useless to the rational planner. Future
libraries will certainly use access in those cases in which the
local collection cannot supply user needs. Libraries have been
giving access to knowledge and information not in their collections for more than a century. Resource sharing and interlibrary
loan may lack the pizzazz of the virtual library, but they are
established and thriving facts of real library life. The balance
between access and collection will differ from library from

library and from subject area to subject area within a library. In most libraries, that balance will shift over time. Realistically, however, future public, academic, and school libraries must base their service on strong local collections, for economic as well as other reasons.

Costs of Electronic Distribution Revisited

The costs[1] set out here, though hypothetical, represent reasonable estimates based on current charges for article delivery services and other known cost factors. The minimal prices that we give do not take into account *either* the issue of predatory publishers *or* the higher per-unit costs that will come from a change from local collections to just-in-time distribution.

Apart from interlibrary loan, the prices and costs do not include staff costs at the library that is acquiring material, even though staff costs represent 40 to 70 percent of a typical library's budget. Our estimates *do* assume that users will need printed copies of any items long enough to involve library acquisition and that publishers will continue to carry out all of their functions (editing, marketing, etc.) other than printing and distribution.

A typical cost of $30 per item (in 1990 dollars) for interlibrary loan appears to be not only reasonable but supported by broad studies.[2] That cost is almost evenly split between lending and borrowing libraries.

For on-demand articles, we will posit a minimum average cost of $10 (1990 dollars) including printing, copyright clearance, and distribution, noting that this average is probably on the low side.

---

1.   It is important to remember the real costs of electronic distribution (discussed in Chapter 6) in order to put real library costs in perspective.

2.   The best recent study is reported in Marilyn M. Roche, *ARL/RLG interlibrary loan cost study: a joint effort by the Association of Research Libraries and the Research Libraries Group*, Washington, D.C.: The Association, 1993.

For book-length items distributed electronically and printed locally on demand, $15 appears to be about as low a figure as could be supported for material protected by copyright, with $10 as a possible minimum figure for out-of-copyright and public domain material.

Public Libraries: The Best Bargain

The American public library system is a unique and uniquely effective part of society, representing a public sector service and a safety net that actually work. The newly unemployed looking for help in writing résumés or mounting job searches; those planning to start small businesses; people attempting home decorating and repair; children learning to associate reading with pleasure; those who need to learn just a little bit about a new topic; and those who want to broaden their horizons with pleasure reading of any stripe—all these and more benefit from the common good of public library collections and services. The short answer to those advocating a shift away from local collections in public libraries is simple—for reasons set out below, such a change makes no economic or societal sense, no matter how cold-eyed the analysis of the figures.

Not Just Facts

The case for virtual libraries—and "access vs. collection"—rests in large part on the overriding importance of data, information, facts—the need to have the very latest stuff at any cost. Anyone who believes in that overriding importance can accept that the virtual library is a good thing because it will provide facts faster and better than a print-based physical library.

The premises are, of course, faulty. Libraries should not be discussing access *vs.* collection, but determining the correct balance of access *and* collection. Even more importantly, no library is merely a place for obtaining up-to-the-minute facts. We estimate that 80 percent of the activity in good public libraries has nothing to do with providing current data. Public libraries serve a range of functions all of them important. Are we to devalue the free circulation of genre fiction (romance novels, mysteries, etc.) to masses of patrons? Story-telling hours and community programs? The importance of the public library *as a place* for older people, children, the unemployed, the disabled, and working people of all kinds? The public library provides a host of valuable services and thereby helps to make the community stronger and improve the overall mental and social health of its people.

What Real Libraries Do

The Redwood City (CA) Public Library spends a quarter of a million dollars a year on literacy programs—which is not the provision of data, just vitally important. In Florida during fiscal 1991–92, public libraries reported holding 75,504 programs with a total attendance of 2,436,218 people—an amazing number for a state in which libraries serve just under 13 million people.[3]

Someone starting with the assumption that a public library is a glorified InfoKiosk will, inevitably, come up with a half-baked electronic "library service." Someone who sees the public library for what it is—a vital and multifaceted part of the community—will realize that it will not and cannot be replaced by electronics.

Real Numbers: Circulating Print Collections

Very few know that almost all public libraries services are a real bargain, perhaps the best bargain of any public agency. In the United States and Canada, public library collections circulate at an effective cost of $1.87 per circulation (1991–92 figures), *even if* it is assumed that all material costs and 60 percent of all other library costs should be allocated to the cost of circulation.[4] There is simply no way you can get that kind of bargain through other means—not if authors and editors are expected

---

3. Derived from *Florida library directory with statistics, 1993/94*, Tallahassee: Department of State, Division of Library Services, 1993.

4. Except as otherwise noted, all figures in this section derive from information in *American library directory 1993–94*, New Providence, N.J.: Bowker, 1994, and exclude New Jersey and Massachusetts.

to eat, not if telecommunications firms are expected to operate, and particularly not if libraries are to meet the public's legitimate, continuing demand to read long texts in print-on-paper.

In 1991–92, U.S. and Canadian public libraries circulated 1.6 *billion* items. In a print-on-demand, electronic-based system, at $10 per item—probably lower than the lowest feasible cost—that would require $16 billion to replace circulating items alone. Sixteen billion dollars is slightly more than *three times the total budgets* of all public libraries in the U.S. and Canada—with nothing left over for reference collections, librarians, programs, or any of the other services that make public libraries worthwhile. Even if present public library budgets doubled, the library would still be an excellent bargain. Collections for circulation alone are simply too cost-effective to give up (even if we ignore, as we should not, in-library use, browsing, reference, and other uses).

What Serials Crisis?

Consider the serials crisis as it affects most public libraries. Serials crisis? What serials crisis? The serial price inflation that has severely afflicted academic libraries is, at worst, a minor issue for public libraries. For most public libraries, the term is meaningless. For example, Florida public libraries spent about 14 cents on serials for every dollar spent on books in fiscal 1991–92.[5] They spent about as much on serials in that year as they spent on microform, audiovisual, and machine-readable items combined. Around the country, public libraries appear to spend no more than 10 to 20 percent of their total materials budgets on serials, and that percentage seems not to be rising.

Consider two price indexes for the serials that public libraries are most likely to hold. The average subscription price for titles indexed in *Magazine Article Summaries* was $43 in 1991 and $48 in 1994—an 11.63 percent increase in four years. Ninety percent of those titles are published in the United States at an average annual subscription cost of $40 in 1994—while

---

5.   Derived from *Florida library directory with statistics.*

the 10 percent published abroad average $117.[6] The numbers
are higher for larger public libraries with comprehensive serials
collections, but still not outrageous. Ebsco's *Serial Price Projections 1995* gives figures for a 3,295-title public library collection. The 3,019 U.S. titles averaged $45.29 in 1990 and $55.81
in 1994, an increase of 23.23 percent over five years (an average
yearly increase that is about the same as general inflation). In
the case of the Ebsco public library list, the 276 non-U.S. titles
are almost comparably priced—at $50.27 in 1990 and $65.04
in 1994 (an increase of 29.38 percent).[7]

Article-on-demand services in place of local collections in
public libraries would substantially reduce the kind of use that
serials receive, as well as massively increasing the cost of each
use. Such a change would represent the worst kind of quack
cure for an imaginary ailment—the kind that kills the patient.

Recognizing All Uses of Library Materials

It is important to include all uses of library materials and
services in order to understand exactly what good value for
money public libraries are. Unfortunately, few public libraries
know how many transactions take place. Only a handful of
libraries measure in-library use effectively, even though some
research shows that, in poor and rural communities, in-library
use can exceed circulation.[8] Florida does provide in-library
estimates.[9] For that state—neither rich nor poor (its per capita
library funding is a little below the national average)—if circulation, in-library use, reference transactions, and program attendance are combined and divided into the total funding for
libraries, the result is $2.50 per transaction, *all* library expenses

6.   Lee Ketcham and Kathleen Born, "Projecting serials costs: banking on the
past to pay for the future," *Library Journal* (April 15, 1994), pp. 44–50.

7.   *Serials price projections 1995*, Birmingham, Ala.: Ebsco Subscription
Services, 1994.

8.   Personal communication from Christie M. Koontz based on research
leading to her article "Public library site evaluation and location: past and
present market-based modelling tools for the future," *Library and Information
Science Research* 14 (1992), p. 379–409.

9.   *Florida library directory with statistics.*

included. That is an incredible bargain by any standard. In California, the average is $2.25 per transaction.[10]

Signs of Robust Library Service

Different public libraries have different needs and different patrons and serve different purposes. Most public libraries have some research collections and services. Some public libraries have substantial community outreach and literacy programs—others struggle just to keep the doors open. First-rate public library service is not cheap in total, although it is still a bargain by any reasonable measure. As Hugh Craig Atkinson said, "Libraries that do a lot, do a lot."[11] In looking at California public libraries, which range from unusually well-funded to barely funded at all, we found some criteria indicative of strong and robust library service. These criteria are not presented as being universally applicable, but they do work in the California context. For example:

◆ Robust public libraries answer more than 2 reference questions per year per person in the entire service population. Strong libraries answer between 1.3 and 2 questions per person. Good reference service is not cheap (nothing that labor-intensive can be), but it keeps the library at the heart of the community.

◆ Robust public libraries circulate more than ten items per year per person in the entire population. Strong libraries circulate between six and ten items per person. Alternatively, considering total *transactions* per capita, robust libraries do at least a dozen transactions per person; strong libraries at least eight.

---

10. California figures derived from *California library statistics 1992/93*, Sacramento: California State Library, 1993.

11. A favorite saying of this great librarian. It indicated his optimistic, expansive view of libraries and his shrewd perception of reality. It is demonstrably true that libraries that develop and organize their collections vigorously will, among other things, circulate materials at a high rate, lend materials to other libraries and borrow from other libraries at a high rate.

♦ Robust public libraries are funded to the tune of at least a
dime a day—that is, operating budgets of $37 or more per
capita per year. Reasonably strong libraries have at least a
nickel a day—that is, per capita annual budgets of $18 and
up. Those numbers will vary widely, to be sure, just as the
cost of living and other costs vary in different regions. The
national average was almost a nickel a day in 1991/92 and
surveys suggest that most people feel it should be more.

♦ Robust libraries (all but the very largest) turn over their
circulating collections at least twice a year. Thus a public
library with holdings of half a million volumes will, if it
is robust, have more than a million circulation transactions a year. These figures make "print on demand" strategies economically infeasible and ridiculously unattrac-
tive. Robust libraries also have programs to replace or
enrich their collections on a continuing basis, so that
patrons have a steady supply of reasonably current materials. In a well-maintained library, at least fifty cents per
circulation should go toward materials—that is the statewide average for Florida, and it appears to be a minimum
figure for strong libraries in other states.

♦ It should go without saying that strong libraries have
strong professional staffs that provide, among other things,
readily available reference service; that strong libraries
buy new books actively and maintain vital serials collections; that strong libraries offer CD-ROM and other digital
services as appropriate to meet their patrons' needs; and
that strong libraries and librarians make their services
known and are energetic and committed in seeking the
funding they need.

Making the Case: A Dime a Day

Libraries of the future should be aggressive in making their case
for strong budgetary support. More people use public libraries
than almost any other public service and those libraries, year
in and year out, offer some of the most cost-effective and valued
service possible. That will not change, *unless* public libraries

lose their way in ill-advised and irresponsible all-digital escapades.

A dime a day (1990 figures, plus inflation)—that is a good starting point for a truly robust library in an economically healthy area. It is an average goal, to be sure, and some of the best and largest libraries should aim higher. An interesting example is Berkeley, California—a city that *loves* its public library and expresses that love to the tune of $76 a year (20 cents a day) per capita. The result is a library that performs extraordinarily well—more than a dozen circulations, almost seventeen transactions, and more than four reference questions per Berkeley resident.

Also in the San Francisco Bay Area, Redwood City funds at $54 a year (15 cents a day) per capita (that does not include some substantial recent capital outlays) even though it is one of the less wealthy communities in a prosperous county. It, too, has high usage—more than ten circulations and almost fourteen transactions per capita (with total transactions probably underreported). Even in California, a dime a day is a dream for most public libraries—the statewide average is less than half that amount. At a dime a day, California's closed libraries could reopen and every library could offer the kind of service that makes for heavily used libraries.

An all-digital future is not the answer for public libraries, although libraries must and will make more use of electronic information and networking. Print collections form the core of today's and tomorrow's libraries. Print circulating collections will continue to be impressive bargains, even in times when libraries finally have enough money to provide the professional service people need and deserve.

Academic Libraries: Finding the Numbers

The term academic libraries covers a wide range of libraries— libraries that differ in terms of size, location, mission, and institution served. Community college libraries serve student populations that reflect the general community. The libraries of small private liberal arts colleges have different missions from those of either community colleges or large research universities. Even considering larger institutions, one finds differences between public and private, large and very large, and the biggest libraries belonging to the Association of Research Libraries (ARL) and next-level libraries. Within ARL, there are huge differences between the largest and the smallest members.

As academic libraries attempt to obtain the kind of funding they need and deserve, they almost all encounter one big problem—the lack of usable output measures, at least on a national scale. By output measures, we mean circulation, in-library use (including reserved-book room use), reference activity (in person and by mail, telephone, fax, etc.), interlibrary lending and borrowing, library instruction activity, user head counts, and any other objective and measurable indications of library use and services.

ARL reports only one output measure—interlibrary loan. So does the Association of College and Research Libraries (ACRL) for the next-largest group of libraries. Nonlibrarian administrators out to save a buck and library administrators pushing the virtual library are materially assisted by this lack of national reports on output measures. If academic libraries could gather and present collective figures that gave a true picture of total library use, the virtual library would be seen as the hollow sham it is; and even the most malignant library-hater would be laughed out of the conference room. If a library does not measure everything that it is doing now, how can it predict the cost-effectiveness of doing things differently? If libraries have no national figures as benchmarks, how can they know what is reasonable?

Such numbers should be available. Most libraries in the 1990s, academic or otherwise, count circulation as a matter of course—automatically, in the case of libraries with automated circulation systems. However, for most academic libraries, circulation does not come near to representing a majority use of library materials. When libraries have counted in-library use, usually omitting pure browsing, the numbers are typically two to three times as high as actual circulation.[12] Such figures comport with the common sense understanding of the research and study habits of students and faculty.

It is burdensome (but by no means impossible) to count all reshelving. It is nearly impossible to determine the amount of in-house use that does not require reshelving. It is also burdensome and complicated to count reference use—one of the most important professional services offered by any library. It is not unreasonable to ask academic libraries, as a minimum, to do one-week counts, say, twice a year (once during the fall term, once during the spring). Such counts could be extrapolated for the entire year by using usage curves that circulation systems can provide. As a first step, academic libraries could take a week in the middle of each semester or quarter and multiply by the number of weeks in the academic year (including summer weeks for an institution with high summer use); although a multiplier based on circulation would give better figures.

For far too long, the only widely reported measures of academic library performance have been those reinforcing the caricature of the library as a "warehouse of books." Any even passable academic library is much more than that caricature. It *is* important to build and maintain collections offering breadth and depth for current and future researchers. It is also important to provide maximum opportunity for today's library users to use those collections. To be effective politically, it is vital to record the totality of collection use.

California: A Case in Point

California is one of the few states providing a number of output measures for many of its academic libraries. We believe the California figures provide useful yardsticks.[13] After analyzing

---

12. Personal communications from a number of academic institutions throughout the country.

13. The following circulation figures, volume counts, subscriptions, reference, and ILL counts are all taken from *California library statistics*, with additional *counted* in-house usage figures provided to Walt Crawford by Liz Gibson, planning consultant for the California State Library. Turnover and circulation per person figures are derived directly from those reports.

direct reports from a number of other institutions and finding that in-library use (although probably generally underreported) was consistently two to three times circulation, we have assigned a nominal figure of 1.5 times circulation for in-library use in public universities.

Obviously, usage levels and transaction costs vary widely between types of academic library and even between academic libraries of the same type. However, as these examples show, academic libraries are not expensive warehouses of little-used and unused books. They contain effective collections that serve their patrons far more economically than any conceivable electronic alternative.

♦ The eight general campuses of the University of California had 159,429 students in the year reported and 17,534 faculty. They all have large libraries (the smallest, UC Santa Cruz, had 1.04 million volumes; the total was 24.5 million for the eight campuses) with large budgets ($141 million total). Total circulation was 6.6 million items (37.5 per person); circulation turnover rate was 27 percent—more than one circulation per year for every four books. The imputed total transactions were 108 per person. Assigning all material expenses, all student wages, and 50 percent of all other expenses to *material* transactions, we have arrived at an average of $5.46 per material transaction—or $7.40 per transaction for all transactions, *covering the entire library budgets*. Turnover rates ran from Berkeley's 20 percent to Santa Cruz's 48 percent—and, if reasonable extrapolations for in-library use are included, even Berkeley has 50 percent annual turnover.

♦ In the year reported, the two largest UC campuses, in terms of collections—7.8 million and 6.2 million volumes—and budgets—$31 and $35 million operating, came out a little below average in cost per transaction. Berkeley was $5.03 per material transaction and $7.17 for all transactions; UCLA $4.29 and $6.09. Then again, Berkeley circulated 45 items per person (125 transactions overall), while UCLA circulated 51 items per person (145 transactions overall)—these are *very* busy libraries. Turnover for those huge collections, *not* including reference and in-library use, was 20 percent for Berkeley, 32 percent for UCLA. Look at that latter number in particular. If UCLA handled all of its circulation (not including in-library transactions) by electronic distribution and printing on demand, using typical current printing techniques, that process would generate almost precisely *as much paper each year as is stored in UCLA's entire collection.* On top of that, assuming a modest $10 per item for *all* transactions, including in-library, the cost would be $58 million—seven times UCLA's current material expenditures and 160 percent of its entire budget, with nothing left for anything except on-demand printing and copyright clearance. Let us repeat:

♦ A "virtual" UCLA library would produce as much paper *every year* as is now contained in the library and involve spending $160 on printing on demand for every $100 now spent on *all library collections, programs, and services.* Anyone for virtuality?

♦ In the same period, the 20 California State University campuses, serving 363,128 students and 17,155 faculty members with a total of $89 million operating expenditures and 14.2 million volumes, had much higher turnover but considerably less usage per person. Total circulation was 7.2 million items (or 18.9 per person); turnover rate was 51 percent—one circulation per year for every two books. Imputed total service was 55 transactions per person. Material transactions averaged $3.28 each; assigning all costs to all transactions results in a $4.27 average. On the individual campuses, turnover ranged from 29 percent to 103 percent; circulation per person ranged from 11 to 37; total transactions ranged from 41 to 98 per person.

♦ A sampling of the libraries of 24 private colleges and universities (including USC but not including Stanford) serving a total of 84,000 students showed an average of 19 circulations per person (7 to 68), with a total of 36 transactions per person (10 to 102, clearly undercounted in some cases). Average cost per material transaction was

$9.19 ($3.03 to $21.86); average fully-burdened cost per transaction overall was $12.04 ($3.90 to $26.08). Private institutions tend to be more expensive to operate. Turnover averaged 21 percent (9 percent to 70 percent).

♦ Only half of California's public junior and community college libraries reported fully enough to make workable calculations.[14] For those 58 campuses (serving 726 thousand students, with $32 million operating expenditures), circulation per person averaged only 3.9, with 5.5 total transactions—but student body size is typically reported in totals, not in full-time equivalents (FTE). Cost per material transaction averaged $5.45 ($3.02 to $14.77); fully-burdened cost per transaction overall was $7.74 ($4.16 to $19.90). Turnover averaged 77 percent (16 percent to 530 percent).

A sample of figures from comparable institutions in other states indicates that their costs and volume of transactions are in the same general ranges.

Usage

It is often said that academic libraries pay too much to store books that are not used.[15] Let us leave aside for now the important argument that very large research collections are *supposed* to have large numbers of volumes that are not currently in demand and may never be heavily used. The solution advanced for the "problem" of storing unused and underused books is to digitize the "information" in those books and provide just-in-time printing. It is certainly true that large academic collections do not have the per volume use of public library collections, but it is easy to overstate the numbers.

In California, community colleges averaged 77 percent turnover; state university campuses averaged 51 percent; and

---

14. Note that many of California's largest community colleges were excluded because of inadequate reporting.

15. See, for example, the notorious "Pitt study": Allen Kent and others, *The use of library materials: the University of Pittsburgh study*, New York: Dekker, 1979.

even the very large University of California campuses had a turnover rate of more than 25 percent of their collections each year on average. A study of in-library use at UC Riverside, one of the smaller of the University of California campus libraries, suggests strongly that those uses cover much of the print collection that does not circulate.[16] This study and others indicate that the supposedly massive "unused collection" is more a folk myth than a modern academic library reality.

A Real Serials Crisis

For most academic libraries, the serials crisis is real. Many journal prices are increasing at a rate well over general inflation; the fluctuating dollar takes its toll; predatory publishers exploit a captive market; and materials budgets have sustained deep cuts. There really is a crisis—but it is neither universal nor simple to analyze. For that matter, the crisis has to be seen as an issue of underfunding as much as of overpricing. For ARL libraries, at least, if the libraries were receiving an appropriate portion of total university expenditure, they would almost certainly be able to maintain the serials collections they need and, at the same time, acquire appropriate numbers of monographs and other materials.

Let us look at the major elements of a reasonably comprehensive university serials collection—that is, one containing all the titles covered by *Arts and Humanities Citation Index*, *Social Science Citation Index*, and *Science Citation Index*. Even by looking at general categories the nature of the crisis appears fairly clear.[17]

♦ **Arts and humanities**: Roughly half the titles come from the United States, half from overseas. The U.S. titles averaged $64 in 1991 and $82 in 1994. Foreign titles went from $133 on average in 1991 to $165 in 1994. In 1994, subscriptions to the comprehensive arts and humanities

16. Jeff Selth, Nancy Koller, and Peter Briscoe, "The use of books within the library," *College & Research Libraries* 53 (May 1992): 197–205.

17. Figures in this section are taken from Lee Ketcham and Kathleen Born, op. cit.

collection cost approximately $191,000—of which two-thirds went for non-U.S. publications. That sum does not indicate a crisis for libraries in comprehensive universities, and it is difficult to justify widespread serial cancellations in the arts and humanities.

♦ **Social sciences:** The costs are higher for these materials. Roughly half of the titles come from U.S. publishers, and these went from an average of $148 in 1991 to $206 in 1994—almost a 40 percent increase in four years from an already high base. Foreign publications averaged $347 in 1991 and $436 in 1994—a 26 percent increase. Again, two-thirds of a comprehensive subscription total would go to non-U.S. publishers, but this time the total list would cost around $790,000: more than *four times* as much as the arts and humanities collection, for less than half again as many titles.

♦ **Sciences:** More science journals come from outside the United States, and here the prices are clearly a major problem. U.S. titles went from $268 in 1991 to $378 in 1994 and foreign titles from a $515 average in 1991 to $666 in 1994 (for each of 1,734 foreign titles). The total list would cost around $1,634,000 (73 percent of that being spent on foreign titles). If the $666 average subscription seems high, consider that the 196 physics journals in the list averaged $1,099 each in 1994 and that the 209 chemistry journals averaged $1,106 each.

The three lists combined would have an annual subscription cost of more than $2.6 million—a massive sum for any library, particularly since there are many relevant journals not listed in these citation indexes.

It is important to note that the arts and humanities represents less than 8 percent of the total cost despite accounting for more than one-quarter of all the titles. Moreover, those titles include many whose back issues are frequently used. Note also that the average cost of an arts and humanities subscription is $68. Given these figures, the publishers of the 338 language and literature journals may well resent being included as a cause of the serials crisis. It is not their doing, by any reasonable measure. Scholars in the arts and humanities also use monographs more heavily than those in some other fields.

Libraries that have imposed across-the-board cuts in serials—and, worse, siphoned money away from monographs to pay for outrageously-priced science journals—have punished the arts and humanities for problems to which they do not contribute. Given the traditional support for libraries among the humanities and arts, this seems to be suicidal behavior.

Costs and Effectiveness

Academic libraries lack effective tools to demonstrate their cost-effectiveness. However, even the crudest models suggest strongly that handling everything electronically is not the answer for those libraries. A massive move to digital just-in-time service would be ruinous, leading to impoverished services for all but a few wealthy researchers—most of whom bypass the library in any case. What do we mean by "ruinous"? We will make it simple, and assume that all of the circulation, reference, ILL, and in-house transactions could be matched by electronic just-in-time means at an average of a very low $10 per transaction *for direct costs*. Note that this figure does *not* include the costs of librarians to help users find, evaluate, and understand sources, nor does it include any other costs.

- ♦ For the libraries of the University of California, Berkeley, that cost alone would have been $43 million for 1991–92— $12 million more than Berkeley's entire operating budget, and *seven times* the library's material expenditures.

- ♦ For the library of the California State University, Fresno, a library with slightly less than one million volumes serving a campus of more than 20,000 students and faculty, the cost would have been $17.8 million—more than *three times* the total operating budget and more than 10 times the materials budget.

- ♦ For the University of Tennessee, Knoxville, library, the cost would have been $15.6 million—almost twice the total operating budget and just under five times the total material budget.

It makes no sense to sum up the significance of a college or university library by totaling its circulation, in-house, and reference usage. However, even by such simplistic measures, and even ignoring the dramatic harm done to students and scholars by ruling out browsing and serendipity, a massive move away from well-maintained collections would cost enormously more than would funding academic libraries at the levels they need and deserve.

Making the Case

The Association of Research Libraries has finally admitted what some observers have suspected—academic library funding *as a percentage of campus expenditures* has been dropping for years, even as subscription costs, the number of journals, book prices, staff costs, etc., have been rising. Such libraries are not getting the 5 percent of total campus expenditures that should be a minimal standard, and they are certainly not getting the 7 percent plus that would be appropriate funding. Instead, the percentages are declining from an average, too-low 3.9 percent in 1982 to a catastrophic 3.32 percent in 1992. Something is terribly wrong here, particularly given the reality that many campus administrations believe, in the face of the facts, that library expenses are inordinately high and growing.

In the typical large academic library, material costs represent between 20 and 30 percent of the total operating budget. If average funding increased from 3.32 percent to 5 percent, libraries could *double* their acquisitions budgets while making moderate increases in other budget lines and thus be on the path to long-term health. Academic libraries should by no means abandon the search for ways to deal with the outrageous prices and publication practices of some serials publishers. However, the nub of the academic library problem is not the iniquitous pricing of some library materials but an inappropriate level of funding.

Each academic library should state its particular mission clearly. That mission statement must be based on the long-term needs of scholarship and the academic program *and* on the immediate needs of students (all students) and faculty. Academic librarians need to understand their users and it is vital that they have the clear and unshakable support of those users if they are to defend themselves against the minority of administrators who see the library as a cost center rather than a center of academic life.

Most researchers will agree that they depend on the library to keep up with the literature of their field. Many researchers browse as a basic aspect of their work. That being so, library collection development and maintenance is a fundamental part of research—and an appropriate proportion (5 to 7 percent) for library operations should be part of every research grant.

Academic libraries (especially the largest, most research-oriented institutions) will see an increased use of electronic resources. With luck, university consortia and other means will be successful in ameliorating the predatory serials pricing that afflicts academic libraries. However, those enhanced resources and new strategies cannot and will not replace print collections or substitute for their development and maintenance—if academic libraries are to survive and continue to contribute to the health of the academy and of society.

The Limits of Access: Libraries Are Not Factories

Those who, in the teeth of reason, peddle the access paradigm make constant use of contemporary industrial analogies. They urge libraries to adopt the "just-in-time" model that has served some factories well and to abandon the "just-in-case" model represented by strong local collections. Most analogies are suspect, but consider that a number of automakers and other industrialists have been hoist on their own "just-in-time" petard in recent years. A brief rail strike shut down many factories because they had no raw materials in reserve. More disturbingly, any number of smaller manufacturers in the personal computer industry were weakened or put out of business because sole suppliers of essential components favored larger

customers when scheduling shipments. The smaller manufacturers had to shut down or pay ruinously higher prices because
they had no reserves. "Just-in-time" works beautifully when
suppliers are totally reliable and when the customer is either
more powerful than the supplier or has a choice of supplier.
Interchangeable parts guarantee a choice of supplier, thus
maintaining the customer's ability to ensure timely delivery.

Libraries are not factories. No library orders thousands of
interchangeable books and journals. Each book and journal
represents a unique entity not replaceable by any other book or
journal. If a scholar needs a particular article in *Science*, the
library can hardly substitute an article of the same length from
Scientific American just because the latter periodical is cheaper.
Even for public libraries, it is condescending and ruinous for a
library to assume that genre fiction may simply be ordered by
the gross. Connoisseurs looking to read all of John D. MacDon-
ald's Travis McGee mysteries are unlikely to regard Lilian
Jackson Braun's "Cat Who . . ." books as appropriate substitutes.
Science fiction readers with eclectic tastes may enjoy Philip
José Farmer, Connie Willis, and Barry B. Longyear equally, but
are unlikely to regard each as interchangeable with the others.

The Madness of Just-in-Time

The just-in-time model fails for libraries *as a general proposition* because supplies are not interchangeable and because
libraries are not, individually at least, more powerful than the
suppliers. For the virtual library to work, the material to which
access is given must come from somewhere. There are several
possible sources and each represents potential problems if the
access paradigm succeeds:

 ♦ Borrowing from larger or more specialized libraries works
   very well (although not inexpensively) as long as there is
   a cooperative framework and the borrowing is matched by
   lending (not in absolute numbers but proportionately). It
   also depends on other libraries *not* adopting the just-in-
   time model that the borrowing library has embraced—that
   is, on there being enough libraries purchasing specialized
   journals and books to ensure that the prices of those items

do not become wholly impossible. Where can the library turn when everyone is busy being hyperefficient?

♦ Acquiring from private publishers through electronic distribution or one-off physical purchase (directly or through a distributor) can work—but it places the library at the mercy of the publisher, who will assuredly charge more for each individual acquisition than for one of a published run, both because the costs are higher and because the publisher knows that the library has no other source.

♦ Acquiring from government-funded or otherwise "free" sources requires a seismic change in the publishing industry and raises some nasty questions about single control of the intellectual apparatus of the country. As discussed earlier, such grand solutions may never work and certainly cannot work without revolutionary change in the country as a whole toward a wholly socialist model—not the most fashionable societal structure of the age.

One partial solution is print-on-demand acquisition of journal articles. That has some promise as a short-term solution *for some journals and some libraries*. There is a trap, however—the price per article is already higher than some can afford and will only stay semi-reasonable as long as publishers still have large subscription bases—and as long as libraries have multiple sources for the documents. We agree with a comment by Charles W. Bailey, Jr.:

> The annual cost of licenses for local electronic databases and access fees for remote commercial resources will grow as the library and its users become more dependent on these electronic resources. In the long-term, if libraries opt for access instead of ownership (e.g., they don't buy selected journals, but pay per article as it's needed), libraries will collectively hold fewer new materials and be more dependent on commercial suppliers.[18]

18. Electronic message on PACS-L, February 18, 1992.

Those suppliers will be benevolent, of course. Look at how hard they have worked to keep the prices of print journals down.

The scheme of relying on larger libraries is also effective—*as a partial, limited solution*. There are two reasons why this is not a comprehensive answer. Larger libraries are also under economic pressures and, in some cases, looking to substitute access for ownership. At some point, the question becomes "access from whence?"—the only answer is either the publisher or some nonexistent universal supply agency. The other problem is that interlibrary lending continues to be expensive, and seems unlikely to become substantially cheaper. If a library borrows a currently-available, reasonably-priced item more than twice, it would probably be cheaper and more efficient to purchase it.

When Access Makes Sense

Access as a code word for the virtual library is a concept without much utility. Access meaning making remote resources available to library users not only makes eminently good sense but has been a common practice since the early days of libraries. That kind of access is based on a mutuality of interest between libraries, not on a fantasy of "essentially free" access to knowledge and information—access without a contribution from the recipient to the general good. That latter fantasy involves, for example, the dissemination of, and subsidized access to, journal articles in electronic form with no payment beyond the cost of printing. Minor details such as the destruction of the print journal publishing industry—the industry that provides the articles in the first place—seem not to bother those who spread the access myth. Here are some examples of access in the good sense of the word:

♦ A developed, coordinated system of resource sharing based squarely on local, regional, state, national, and international cooperation (in that order) and on the ready availability of electronic bibliographic databases. Such a system would support interlibrary lending and borrowing

(physical document, fax, and electronic) based on cooperative acquisition and preservation policies at each level
from local to international.

♦ Cooperatively created and maintained electronic databases of specialized materials such as government documents, technical reports, etc., providing online access to
data and short texts in the public domain to all library
users.

♦ Image (including cartographic) and video databases created and maintained by public consortia to provide access
to these materials to all library users.

None of these examples of "good" access can be or should be
based on the payment of end-user fees. They should be created
and maintained by groups of public, academic, school, and
special libraries, working, where appropriate, with national
libraries and other national agencies on the basis of propor-
tional contributions (money and human resources) and universal availability of the services. The keys are **cooperation** and
availability to all users, regardless of their means.

Balancing Collection and Access

Each library must adopt and maintain a policy of continuously
monitoring the balance between collection and access. There
are no universal rules or mandated ratios. While one library
may reasonably hope to fill 95 percent of its users' needs for
materials by means of its local physical collection, another
library may find it more appropriate to aim at a 50 percent ratio
from its collection, particularly if a substantial portion of the
remaining 50 percent is available electronically.

With almost no exception, any library that abandons its
collection in favor of electronic access as a sole solution will
cease to be a library. On the other hand, any library that expects
to provide all of its users' needs from its own collection is also
doomed. Sensible librarians know their libraries need both
strong collections and a system that delivers materials not
owned. They also know that the balance between the two will

change continuously. It is important that balance be maintained based on the resources of the locality (in the first instance) and the real needs of the library's users, not on some ideology-based target for would-be "libraries of the future."

Points to Remember

📖 Public libraries with strong circulating collections represent incredible bargains and are some of the most effective publicly funded agencies.

📖 Well-funded public libraries serve their communities best. "A dime a day" ($36.50 per capita funding) should be a national average goal.

📖 Academic libraries need nationally reported measures of output—circulation, reference, and in-house usage—to make their economic cases.

📖 Academic libraries have been losing relative funding and need to work with their faculty, researchers, and students in order to reverse that trend.

📖 Objective usage figures demonstrate that academic libraries are not "warehouses for unused dead trees" and that they operate more economically than would electronic equivalents.

10

Survival Guide to the Serials Crisis

L ibraries are diverse and complicated. There is no one library problem—though underfunding approaches universality—so there cannot be one library solution. We need many strategies and solutions if we are to survive and prosper. We also need to be mature enough to accept that multiplicity and flexible enough to accept the need for continuing modification of plans. Above all, we need to understand that library life is a continuing struggle to grow and serve, not a conundrum with a straightforward answer. This is particularly true of the serials crisis.

We have already indicated that one of the most difficult problems facing academic libraries today is the dramatic increase in number and price of commercially published scientific, technological, and medical (STM) scholarly journals. Those in the social sciences are a lesser problem. STM journals are at the heart of the serials crisis. That crisis is the result of a number of related problems rather than a single problem, although the size and arrogance of the handful of big international scholarly journal publishers does make an obvious target. It seems to us that the major candidates for alternatives to traditional print subscription are *problem journals*—expensive, little-read titles that are so profitable for publishers and so deleterious for academic libraries.

Problem journals include those so rarely used in a library that purchasing articles as needed, even at $30 an article, is a bargain. Journals with no real subscriber base except libraries may be problems, as may those charging substantial premiums for library subscriptions. Other candidates include journals with an unusually high price per page and narrowly focused journals with high production costs resulting in high prices.

Dealing with Problem Journals

Having identified problem journals, how should libraries deal with them? A number of solutions—not all technological—have been proposed and we may need to use each of them as appropriate.

Move from the Profit
to the Nonprofit Sector

One answer for needed but overpriced journals with substantial communities of interest is to replace them with nonprofit print equivalents. Such a decision may be difficult politically. However, many of the most important scholarly journals in some fields are published by associations—at fair prices that make reasonable profits to support other association activities. Unfortunately, some associations have turned their publications over to commercial publishers—a move that puts libraries back into the same old bind. In some cases, the agency should be the university itself, absorbing not only editorial work (as is usually now the case) but also production and copy-editing work as part of institutional overhead. That is really cost-shifting but if, for example, a journal only needs a quarter-time production manager, it can result in significant savings.

Print on Demand

The most highly touted solution for problem journals is to print articles on demand from electronic databases—a solution that leaves the journals in the hands of their present publishers. We have discussed this partial, problematic solution in Chapter 9.

Rationalizing Print

If STM journals are going to continue to be published in print from the commercial sector, desktop techniques should be substituted for traditional typesetting. For most journals, true desktop publishing and sensible production choices are the most cost-effective ways to achieve high-quality results. It is perfectly possible to eliminate half or more of a publication's costs by examining and rationalizing its production techniques.

Electronic Journals

When rationalized, print journals are a reasonable, but not the only, solution. A number of electronic journals are being issued today and a few have established solid reputations. Realistically, electronic dissemination is not the total answer for a properly refereed and properly edited journal—but, for some, it is a start.

Electronic journals will fail eventually if they are just a means of *distributing* the production costs. If it turns out that most electronic journal subscribers really want most of what is in each issue and, consequently, download and print each issue, electronic distribution will mean a net *increase* in economic and ecological costs—no less real for being hidden. In such a case, each subscriber is using a relatively expensive way to acquire a single copy.

Databanks

An as yet untested solution to the serials crisis is the article databank. In such a system, articles are received, refereed, and, when found acceptable, added to an electronic database. They are listed in electronic indexes and WAIS servers but are not part of a journal and never see the light of day until requested— at which point they are retrieved and read on screen or printed. The idea is certainly feasible technically but has potential drawbacks. Who will pay for, maintain, and guard the databanks? Who will decide what is added? Who will ensure the long-term preservation of individual articles and the system as a whole?

Perish Publishing

Finally, the solution for many articles contained in problem journals is to alter radically the publish-or-perish paradigm. A true emphasis on quality over quantity and a thorough overhaul of the value- and reward-systems in American academia would solve much of the serials crisis. Let us face it, some journals really do not contain anything for which anyone has much, if any, use—the articles in them exist for reasons extraneous to scholarship and the editorship may be more of an ego trip than a disinterested service to truth.

The Dangers of Grand Solutions

Individual and collective efforts to cope with problem journals should, in the long run, meet with success. Scholars, universities, and societies may well be able to create valuable and prestigious new journals that attract the best papers away from commercial publishers. This will be a long process and success may be incremental—yielding significant savings only after many years. Many scholars and administrators find this kind of piecemeal progress unsatisfactory and yearn for a Grand Solution—one that will transform scholarly publishing overnight.

One such solution would replace commercial journal publishing with university-run electronic distribution, with large research universities at the heart of the system. The bedrock of this proposition is that Association of Research Libraries (ARL) libraries currently spend $350 to $400 million each year on commercially published journals so that the universities can retrieve the scholarship that those universities create in the first place. The idea is that, by replacing commercial journal publishing with a consortial electronic distribution system, the amount spent each year could be reduced to $35 to $40 million.[1] The premise might be true and the solution feasible, *if* all of the following assumptions are true:

♦ Serials expenditure in American university libraries ($400 million plus) is entirely on scholarly journals.

♦ Scholarship is a closed, tight-knit universe. All worthwhile articles in scholarly journals are written by scholars employed by American universities, and the only people who need to read those articles are the same scholars.

♦ Universities will accept this closed-universe model; see commercial publishers as mere parasites on the mighty body of American university scholarship (the only worthwhile scholarship in the world); and make the necessary changes in tenure, dealing with copyright issues, etc., etc.

Alas for this world view, according to *Science and Engineering Indicators*, only 22 to 45 percent of science papers come from the United States. According to one informed estimate, 90 percent of American research and development is done in institutions other than universities.[2] Let us assume that 30 percent of scholarly articles come from America and half of those articles come from universities. It follows that the grand proposal to remove all university scholarly papers from print journals will result in a 15 percent reduction in the flow of manuscripts to these journals. Indeed, sampling a few journals published by major international publishers shows just such results: from 6 to 20 percent of the articles in the few journals sampled came from American academic sources.

Now comes the interesting part—who will persuade university scholars that they can or should do without the other 85 percent of papers and that they should tolerate being ex-

---

1.   One version of this Grand Solution is limited to ARL institutions. In order for the solution to have a chance of working, it would have to include all American universities. In that case both the $350–$400 million and the $35–$40 million figures would increase—the latter more than the former.

2.   Advisory Panel for Scientific Publications, "The cost effectiveness of science journals," *Publishing Research Quarterly* 3 (Fall 1992), p. 75.

cluded from world-class print journals? If they remain unpersuaded (as we would bet they will), the result of this glorious experiment would be to *add* a $35 to $40 million boondoggle, *increasing* library costs by a minimum of another 10 percent, with no discernable effect on commercial scholarly journals.

What of other plans to transform scholarly communication through concerted university action? Charles A. Schwartz of Rice University wrote a thoughtful, well-researched and fairly conclusive paper on this subject. His conclusion? "Prospects for restructuring the scholarly communication system are nil."[3] Though he is not pessimistic, Schwartz is realistic and convincing. He calls for gradualism, a call that we would enthusiastically second. Libraries and universities should take practical steps to improve the STM situation and set aside the grand scenarios—they will not work.

Protecting Intellectual Property

The question of intellectual property is at the heart of the scholarly communication issue. In particular, it seems to us that an important part of the resolution of the serials crisis is for scholars to cease to allow themselves to be exploited by the publishers of the journals for which they write. Why do scholars give away rights that free-lance writers will not even sell— and why do universities allow this to happen? This is *not* a general copyright issue. There is nothing wrong with the idea of copyright, even in an electronic era. What is wrong is how scholars treat copyright.

The facts are straightforward. Most scholarly journals take all rights to submitted papers, even though few such journals pay for contributions. When a paper is accepted by a journal, the author either signs a form explicitly assigning copyright to the publisher or has already implicitly agreed to such an arrangement thanks to a statement in the contribution guidelines. University lawyers could raise questions about the latter

---

3.   Charles A. Schwartz, "Scholarly communication as a loosely coupled system: reassessing prospects for structural reform," *College & Research Libraries* (March 1994), p. 111.

form of copyright assignment—but that is not a central issue. The point is that scholars typically give up their intellectual property rights for the privilege of being published in a particular journal. That means that they may not contribute the article to a nonprofit anthology without clearance from the publisher. It means that they may not, legally, post the paper for electronic distribution after it has been accepted. That is just the way publishing is, right? Wrong. It is a neat little con game devised by scholarly publishers.

Out in the real publishing world, for many (if not most) periodicals, it does not work that way. Those periodicals have "first North American serial publication rights" or "one-time publication rights" or, in a form that is harder on the author, "first publication rights." None of these involve assignment of copyright. Typically, authors hold copyright in everything they publish but assign specific rights to the use of their work. Some of these assignments may be broad and long-term but rarely do writers assign rights in perpetuity. Free-lance writers can, and do, sell an article again in a different market, maybe but not necessarily after rewriting it. The author can republish the article in an anthology, post it on the networks, etc., without violating the law or opening the possibility of suit. Free-lance writers get paid for these limited rights assignments. Otherwise, the contract would not be valid—without reward, there is no contract. For the scholar—leaving aside the intangibles of disseminating ideas and gaining academic prestige—the reward is, presumably, free copies and/or free offprints.

Purchase of one-time publication rights is certainly not universal. Some publications do buy all rights, or at least start out with that as a bargaining position. Many book publishers start out with contracts that, to put it kindly, favor the publisher—but they know full well that their knowledgeable authors will negotiate those contracts, and some clauses are easily negotiable. Note the copyright statement on this book. The underlying contract provides that all rights will revert to the authors if the book goes out of print. When a regular edition of a book has status or profit potential, any reputable publisher will agree to such a reversion clause, even if it is not part of their "standard" contract.

Some extraordinarily foolish things have been written about the need to streamline or eliminate copyright for the sake of efficient communication. One statement is that we should shorten copyright to five or ten years—after all, any income from a book is going to be within that period in any case, is it not? Long ago, a professor of biochemistry wrote a science fiction trilogy. He made not a dime in royalties for the first decade, because the first publisher was undercapitalized and ethically deficient. That professor, Isaac Asimov, eventually made more than a million dollars from those books—*The Foundation Trilogy*. His was an extreme case but not unique. The early works of hundreds of authors enjoy lucrative second or, even, third lives. The problems are not with copyright—they are with how it is used and abused.

Steps for Scholars and Authors

If scholars are to gain a measure of control of scholarly communication and, thus, take an important step toward alleviating the serials crisis, they should not agree to assignment of copyright. It is that simple. The most important journal in library automation has a standard copyright form that assigns copyright but permits the author to reuse the article in his or her own publications—but it also has an alternate form, available on request, that grants first-time serial rights and anthology rights to the journal, while retaining copyright and other rights for the author, who only has to ask. If an alternate form is not available, there are many books on writing and publishing that contain suitable language for such agreements.

If the journal has a statement that all submissions imply assignment of copyright, manuscripts should be submitted with a statement that explicitly removes that implication and substitutes a first-serial-publication assignment. What does the scholar have to lose? If the article is important enough to the journal, they will work with the writer. If their rights handling is more important to them, surely the scholar must have a good alternative outlet. If not, maybe it is time to work with the university, or a professional association, to start one.

If a large percentage of the important scholars and writers in any field insist on fair publication contracts, the journals will agree. What choice would they have? This recommendation is neither revolutionary nor unreasonable. It is simply asking that journals play fair. *Los Angeles Magazine* pays up to $2,000 for a 3,500 word article, and what it gets for that is first North American serial rights. Period. What makes a scholarly journal so much more powerful? Why do scholars let themselves be mistreated in this manner?

The Campus Strategy

Many magazines own the copyright on much of what they publish. That is because much of the magazine is written by staff members as work done for hire. As such, it is not the intellectual property of the staff members. It is commonly the case that scholars use university resources to prepare scholarly articles in the field that they are paid to pursue and do much of the research and writing on what could be considered university time. It would not be unreasonable to regard this as work for hire. It would also, therefore, not be unreasonable for the university to claim that the material should be copyrighted *in the university's name*. It seems to us that the university, once alerted properly to the problems of scholarly publishing, would be a much stronger advocate than individual scholars.

Is this far-fetched? Not necessarily. Most research universities now require that scholars sign patent agreements—anything patentable that scholars develop with university resources or that is related to their work at the university belongs to the university. Patents expire faster than do copyrights. Most scholars may not care, but when a scholar writes a first-rate popularization of the field, one that could be worth $30,000 a year in royalties from a commercial publisher, and the university says that it owns that as well, then the scholar may be more alert to the situation. One way to fend off work-for-hire agreements, at least, is to be responsible shepherds of intellectual property rights. Scholars should not squander those rights, particularly by forfeiting them to agencies that are demonstrably destroying libraries' ability to serve the academic community.

Points to Remember

📖 Libraries need incremental strategies and solutions for current and future problems, including the serials crisis.

📖 "Problem journals" can be identified and strategies to deal with them can be devised.

📖 If libraries and institutions wish to target print for electronic replacement, they should choose intelligently and start out small.

📖 While universities and libraries should look for incremental ways to deal with overpriced science, technical, and medical journals (the heart of the "serials crisis"), it is clear that forced conversion to electronic publication by a university consortium is neither feasible nor desirable.

📖 Scholarship is not a closed universe. American universities are not simply "buying back their own scholarship" when their libraries subscribe to scholarly journals.

📖 Scholars should protect their copyrights. Assignment of copyright is not general practice in magazine and trade book publishing, and should not be considered standard practice for scholarly publishing.

📖 Should scholars fail to assert and protect their intellectual property rights, universities may well assert that many scholarly articles are actually work done for hire, with copyright going to the institutions.

11

Future Libraries:
Beyond the Walls

A "library without walls" makes no sense as a replacement for a real library. However, today's and future libraries must continue to reach *beyond the walls*. Libraries of today and tomorrow:

♦ will increasingly offer services to remote users as well as users in the library, although probably never quite as effectively;

♦ must continue to seek innovative ways to provide access to information and materials not locally held, although the physical collection will continue to be a primary tool;

♦ need to adopt tools and techniques that will make extended libraries work, and work well. There are many such tools already in existence and many more will evolve in the years to come.

There will be many different tools—specific solutions for problems and challenges. Libraries can and should continue to find appropriate ways to go beyond the walls, whether it be through rapid material delivery services, electronic reference service, or other techniques involving various levels of technology.

Tools for Improving Access

Effective use of technology and adherence to standards have been crucial in improving library efficiency, enhancing library services, and increasing access to library materials. In order to supplement their local collections, libraries and library users clearly need better access to more materials and more nonmaterial data and information. In many cases, libraries also need to provide better access to their own collections.

Beyond the Local Catalogue: Eureka and FirstSearch

The remarkable spread of online catalogues says a great deal about library use of standards and effective use of technology. Were it not for Z39.2 (the standard underlying MARC), there would never have been the thousands of online systems that contribute so significantly to library services.

More libraries are building on their online catalogue in a number of ways. One important extension of the online catalogue is access to the major elements of the national bibliography—the great databases listing the collections of libraries around the country. Eureka (from RLG) and FirstSearch (from OCLC) provide just that access, at moderate prices and using techniques that serve infrequent searchers well.

Each tool provides single-source searching to collections of more than 23 million (Eureka) and 29 million (FirstSearch) titles in its primary bibliographic files. Each provides optional access to wide ranges of article citation files for additional fees. Each offers subscription pricing for predictable fees as well as per-search pricing to suit smaller institutions. Each works over the Internet—thereby providing cost-effective telecommunications for a growing number of libraries. These are sensible and economical tools. Any academic or substantial public library that truly cares about extended access should have both Eureka and FirstSearch as part of its end-user search services. Smaller libraries should consider using FirstSearch.

Some Internet-happy folk have suggested that libraries should avoid FirstSearch and Eureka, because they carry charges, and should route user searches automatically through all the Internet-accessible online catalogues around the country, "for free." This is nonsense. For one thing, such use of the Internet represents extremely inefficient resource usage, helping to create the traffic jams that are already beginning to occur on the I-way. If continued unchecked, such misuse will almost certainly result in the narrowing of Internet access, as system administrators recognize the load being placed on their systems. For that matter, such automatic searching is a terrible use of the user's time. Repeating a search in several hundred different catalogues, then massaging the results, will inevitably be considerably slower than searching Eureka and FirstSearch. Additionally, some of the most valuable resources in Eureka and FirstSearch come from libraries that do *not* have, and may never have, Internet-accessible catalogues. These include the United Nations, archives, museums, and many special libraries of different kinds.

Eureka and FirstSearch are model applications of technology resulting in inexpensive searches that yield a rapid picture of available resources and where to find them—a rational use of both Internet and computer resources. Fantastical, would-be money saving schemes involving hundreds of searches (on catalogues with a wide variety of search commands and strategies) are the antithesis of the rational use of technology.

Regional Solutions: Secondary Online Catalogues

Is providing access to a variety of online catalogues necessarily a bad idea? As the solution to access to the bibliographic universe it is neither efficient nor particularly sensible. There are circumstances, though, in which access to individual online catalogues is very useful. More and more libraries will (and should) be involved in local and regional consortia with special access provisions. In those cases, access to the other online catalogues—or, better yet, to a real or virtual online union catalogue—makes eminently good sense. Even without formal agreements, libraries and their patrons frequently make use of the other libraries in an area. Access to the catalogues of those libraries is clearly desirable. Also, scholars can make effective use of specific online catalogues when they are planning research travel—although it would be impractical to have all those catalogues on a menu just to meet such a need.

Regional catalogues and other secondary online catalogues can serve various overlapping communities of interest. There will be more regional academic clusters and statewide union catalogues at the college and university level—but there should also be more urban area union catalogues that combine public library and academic holdings, with mutual borrowing privileges. There are already a significant number of true multitype union catalogues, combining not only academic and public, but also school and (sometimes) special libraries. With luck and good will, there will be more.

Where a library user is directed for improved access depends on the specific needs of that user. Whether using a secondary catalogue makes sense at all also depends on the user. It is axiomatic that users should turn to their own institution's collection *first*. The local catalogue always offers fewer problems with information overload. In addition, for many users and uses the real need is for something that can be consulted or borrowed *right now*—not for the newest sources or a comprehensive list of sources.

The University of California MELVYL system is one of the largest and best systemwide online catalogues, but most UC campuses also have their own catalogues and sensible users start there. Increasingly, users should be able to search both local and secondary catalogues from the same terminal. In the not-too-distant future, they will be able to *extend* a search from the local catalogue to secondary and union catalogues and on to Zephyr (Eureka via Z39.50) or FirstSearch in Z39.50 mode by executing fairly straightforward commands. In general, that progression should be predefined, subject to being overridden by the user.

CD-ROM as Union Catalogue and Backup Catalogue

An online catalogue is not the only partial solution for regional access. The CD-ROM union catalogue is a medium that public librarians have adopted as a practical solution. In order to be a cost-effective measure, a CD-ROM union catalogue must be in a situation in which connectivity is a problem and status information is not essential. The latter in particular ensures that it is not a full solution, but in many cases, it is the most appropriate partial solution for today. True technojunkies disdain CD-ROM as an interim medium that has outlived its usefulness and should vanish; after all, it is only an effective real-world solution to specific real-world problems.

Another good use for CD-ROM, for some libraries, is as a backup mechanism—either to provide not quite current access to materials if the online catalogue is down (an increasingly rare occurrence) or, using relatively inexpensive writable CD-ROM, as a good way to back up the system periodically.

Uniform and Diverse Access: Z39.50

Z39.50, the search and retrieval protocol, is a relatively new and still-developing standard that is making expanded access more powerful and more flexible.[1] Ideally, Z39.50 makes it possible for users of a given library catalogue to search remote systems using the commands and menus of their home catalogue and having the results displayed in the same format.

Z39.50 is a reality—Penn State, to take one example, has been searching RLIN databases using Z39.50 since early 1993. RLG's Eureka search service is itself a Z39.50 client speaking to the same Z39.50 server that Penn State uses remotely. Some libraries already benefit from the multiple-server aspects of Z39.50, using their local catalogue user interfaces to search their own collections and other databases. That usage will certainly increase. What has not yet transpired, but will in the near future, is a multiple-client approach—specialized user interfaces providing access to a range of Z39.50 servers and databases. When it comes to user interfaces, individual libraries and their users have different needs and preferences. What better way to satisfy those needs and preferences than with customized Z39.50 clients?

---

1. Commentaries on the ongoing development of Z39.50 appear in *Information Standards Quarterly* and the *LITA Newsletter*, and elsewhere from time to time.

Some day soon, a library automation company will release a truly robust, well-designed Z39.50 client running under Windows 3.x, Windows NT, OS/2, NeXTStep, Solaris, or the Macintosh System 7, or running as a character-based system on DOS. At the same time, the company will produce a fine online catalogue that has its own server on another PC on a local area network, but is set up so that the PC-based clients can also work with other servers in a cost-effective manner. If that company or another also provides a robust Z39.50 server for CD-ROM stacks, an incredibly powerful new wave of automation for small and medium-sized libraries will occur. Contemporary personal computers have more than enough power to make this vision feasible. Once it happens, it will open flexible and powerful capabilities to a much wider range of libraries.

Better Access to Book Collections

Libraries have been adept at developing and adopting tools to improve access to collections, up to a point. Tens of thousands of libraries provide online catalogues, most offering better access to books and other whole items than the card catalogues that preceded them. Thousands of libraries use CD-ROM and locally-mounted article index databases to improve access to the contents of their serials collections.

The stumbling block, to date, has been inadequate access to chapters in books. That includes collections of articles and proceedings, and also many books written as encyclopedic treatments rather than single linear texts. The central issue is conversion of printed text—chapter titles, etc.,—to machine-readable form and creation of subject and name access points. A number of suggested solutions have been considered: adding tables of contents to searchable online records; adding index entries to these records; and assigning more than one classification number to indicate contents. To date, none of these methods has been attempted on a large enough scale to demonstrate its effectiveness in a multidisciplinary collection or to have any real impact on access. Common sense suggests that adding index entries, quite apart from the cost of conversion, may create the kinds of retrieval difficulty that makes full-text retrieval so unwieldy. When applied to tens or hundreds of thousands of books, searchable indices will create enough noise to rival the Indianapolis 500.

Searchable entries in contents lists, on the other hand, have considerable promise *if* a cost-effective way to add and share these entries can be found. The time is ripe for a cooperative program to build shared or downloadable databases that will provide access to collections in book form comparable to current periodical literature access (including authoritative name and subject access). Many library users would be served best by reading part of a book as an introduction to a new topic, but too often wind up reading less useful articles because they are more accessible. It is entirely possible that serious development of such databases has been slowed by the futurists' claim that books are obsolete. If that is so, it is way past time for librarians to recognize the fallacy in that claim and to treat books as the continuing resource they are.

Article Access and Delivery

Article-level access can serve two different functions: improving access to a library's own collection (some of which may be in microform, on CD-ROM, or available in some other non-print form) and expanding available resources by providing articles not held locally. The past few years have seen a proliferation of article delivery systems and tools to support such systems.

CitaDel, UnCover, EPIC

Article-level databases are not new solutions to access problems. Dialog and its competitors have been with us for many years; there are hundreds of abstracting and indexing services available through a variety of means. Some libraries have mounted high-use citation databases (such as the Information Access Company's *Expanded Academic Index*) on local computers; in the last decade, thousands of libraries have provided CD-ROM access (stand-alone or locally networked) to those databases.

Recently, nonprofit library organizations have provided access to citation and serial table-of-contents files, usually over the Internet and usually in conjunction with article delivery systems. The largest of these services are OCLC's set of databases available through EPIC or FirstSearch; RLG's CitaDel files available through Eureka and Zephyr; and UnCover/UnCover II, originally part of CARL. Each of these services has its own strengths and weaknesses. Each provides a table-of-contents service and fee-based article delivery. Two of the three overlap to some extent with Dialog, Mead, and other commercial online services, but also provide their own distinctive citation sources.

Had the rhetoric of some academic librarians in the last decade been prophetic, article delivery systems should now be booming—delivering many thousands of articles every day. The systems provide easy document ordering, fast delivery, prices as low as copyright and other problems will permit, and the kind of citation and delivery combination it is said that library users really need. To date, this kind of document delivery has not become omnipresent. It is hard to know what to make of that.

The fault may lie partly in the failure to distinguish between rhetoric and reality. The rhetoric is that scholars need specific articles right away, and will pay to receive them immediately. The reality may well be that most scholars do not treat most articles as *essential* research material. They are perfectly willing, in most instances, to wait a few weeks for an interlibrary loan—or even to do without the articles that are not actually in the building.

These systems can, nonetheless, be a useful part of the complex access structure that is evolving. There is a potentially lethal flaw, though. If manuscripts continue to flow to journals to which fewer and fewer libraries subscribe, we can confidently predict that the publishers will see to it that document delivery prices go up enough to assure *at least* as much profit as was obtained from selling print subscriptions. This will not save the library community any money.

That is a long-term threat and one that assumes article delivery to be a comprehensive solution. Remember, no solution can be assumed to be permanent and no single solution will solve any complex problem.

Ariel: Efficient Article Delivery

One significant tool is designed to support all article delivery systems, including that of RLG, the tool's developer. Ariel, now available as a Windows application, combines off-the-shelf, competitively-priced devices into a system that provides more than the sum of the devices themselves. Ariel is a document transmission system—a moderately-priced piece of software that runs on a networked personal computer attached to the Internet and can drive a scanner, a laser printer, or both.

The promotional slogan that Ariel "out-faxes the fax" is true in a fairly crude sense, but what Ariel really does is a lot better than that sounds. With efficient data transmission and relatively little effort, it produces output that compares favorably with good photocopies. Ariel was developed by RLG, and is sold by RLG, but it has no direct linkage to the RLIN network or to RLIN data. Ariel transmission should turn up as an option in every document delivery system, including those discussed above. Unlike centralized article delivery systems, Ariel can also be used for library-to-library transmission to take advantage of library fair-use rights.

Again, Ariel is not a total or permanent solution to anything. It certainly does not solve all long-term access problems. Someone has to scan material to an Ariel station (or send it from digital storage). While Ariel resolves timing and print-quality issues (although not for color materials), it does nothing for copyright problems, material that cannot be photocopied because of fragility, or material that no library owns because everybody depended on others to preserve copies. It is a good tool, not a miracle cure.

Access to Enhance Collections

Access to the holdings of other libraries and to electronic resources *enhances* local collections—it does not replace them. For decades, libraries have provided such access and have been engaged in a continuing process of making it more effective. The expanded access of the future will have an increasing component of access to electronic resources—but will not be confined to electronic access. A scholar visiting a special collection in another library; a suburban resident being given borrowing privileges in the city public library—both are examples of expanded access. In hundreds of thousands of cases, familiar interlibrary loan—mailing a book from one place to another—based on shared electronic catalogues, provides expanded access to needed materials. In the case of local (urban and rural), state, and regional alliances, the principal appropriate technology for expanded access will be delivery vans and bookmobiles—not as glamorous to the techie as electronic networks but valuable to and valued by the people they serve.

Forging Alliances to Extend Collections

The key to effective extended libraries is alliance-building. This is recognized by all but those few who still believe that everything will be transmitted electronically from some universal central repository. Libraries and library users will continue to use physical materials and to take advantage of fair-use provisions for photocopying. Therefore, alliances that directly extend a library's collections and services are vital.

Cooperative library ventures have existed effectively for many decades. What is new is the creation of innovative alliances to serve different needs—for example, multitype consortia with mutual borrowing privileges within an urban area. Extending network access through such consortia and providing second-level online catalogue or CD-ROM access to the collections of the members of the consortium make good use of technology for more effective libraries. Even multitype cooperation is not new, though it is still comparatively rare. Such cooperation is not simple and usually has to overcome complex political and financial obstacles. Nevertheless, a geographically-oriented multitype cooperative can be effective in ways that cooperative arrangements between libraries of a single type cannot.

A keen library user would love to live in a community in which a library card provided access (either physically or through fast lending) to the public library, the community college library, the local state university library, school libraries, the nearby private college library, the law libraries of major local law firms, and corporate libraries of the leading businesses. Such is the ideal outcome of the kind of grass-roots cooperation that leads to true expanded access. Multitype cooperation can result in many different solutions to different problems. A union CD-ROM catalogue on which interlending is based may well be the best solution for some localities. Online union catalogues make sense elsewhere. Some consortia may find it feasible to create a universal borrowing card. Cooperation might mean nothing more than librarians from the libraries in the area getting together to discuss mutual problems and their solutions.

Book Vans and Other Appropriate Technology

The great benefit of settling for complexity and a multiplicity of partial solutions is that libraries and library alliances can use *all* the tools at hand to make progress. Appropriate tools and techniques need not be discarded just because they are familiar and low-tech. The state of Illinois has been a leader and has done wonderful work in providing library services through cooperative endeavor. The underpinning of this statewide effort was originally an ancient online system (LCS) that had few merits other than delivering status information on hundreds of thousands of titles held in hundreds of libraries. It was replaced after years of service. The current system is based on a combination of online union catalogues (not terribly advanced) and some very low-tech delivery mechanisms, namely book vans. The Illinois experience was the result of the use of real-world tools and techniques by an alliance of the State Library, all the state-supported academic libraries, and public and multitype library systems. Cooperation and realism are the foundation stones of future library service.

The Illinois solution is, of course, anathema to the techno-junkie. A properly high-tech system would require that all the books in all the libraries be digitized and their contents delivered on demand to desktop readers. It might be faster—but only when everything was in digital form and only if library users found the reading devices acceptable. Libraries in this Anti-Illinois could devote all the money being spent on book vans and the union catalogue to digitizing. After a few decades, they would have made some slight progress. Meanwhile, of course, the citizens of Illinois would not have the slightly delayed access that they have now.

Illinois is an exemplar for the nation because it is solving *today's* problems for *today's* readers using tools at hand, while, at the same time, some Illinois institutions are doing intriguing experiments for the future. That is the way to run libraries and consortia of libraries—search the sky, but keep checking out the books.

Maintaining the Mix

Libraries will and should continue to use a mix of book and other linear document collections, paper journal subscriptions, electronic network-based distribution, full-text CD-ROM, CD-ROM indexes with full-text microfiche, tape-loaded databases, Eureka and CitaDel, EPIC, FirstSearch and OCLC delivery services, UnCover, Dialog, Nexis, and others. The mix changes constantly and will continue to change. Some services may disappear or themselves change; some systems as yet undreamed of may emerge and enrich the mix. There is no reason to believe that any single service—*or any single technology*—will or should take over all libraries. Different technologies are valuable in different situations and libraries are as various as the populations they serve.

Points to Remember

📖 A library should use all available methods to provide service outside the library.

📖 Major national databases (FirstSearch and Eureka) are cost effective enhancements to the service provided by the library's online catalogue. Use of the Internet to consult hundreds of individual online catalogues is neither efficient nor cost-effective.

📖 CD-ROM union catalogues and backup catalogues can be real-world, cost-effective solutions for some libraries and library systems.

📖 In the near future, through the use of Z39.50, library users will be able to extend online catalogue searches to secondary and union catalogues and on to the national databases.

📖 Libraries must cooperate to build shared databases giving access to parts of books (chapters, papers, etc.) at a level commensurate with current journal article access.

📖 Centralized article delivery systems, though useful, have not lived up to the hype in the late 1980s.

📖 The most important element of enhanced library service is cooperation. Effective library alliances use a variety of real-world tools and techniques while continuing to experiment.

12

Successful Libraries Make Their Own Luck

A library should be the heart of a city. With its storehouse of knowledge, it liberates, informs, teaches, and enthralls. A library indeed should be the cultural center of any city. Amidst the bustle of work and commerce, the great libraries of the world have provided a sanctuary where scholars and common man alike come to enlarge and clarify knowledge, to read and reflect in quiet solitude.

Rudolfo Anaya

There will only be successful libraries in the future—because, if libraries are not successful, they will cease to exist. The successful library will be a warm, enriched, enriching place. It will be a haven of civilized values; a place that is dedicated to serving humankind by embracing all the means by which we communicate and using each of those means appropriately. The library will continue to be inclusive and hospitable to diversity—of people, of materials, and of the services it provides. From a child with a picture book to a researcher in an esoteric area to an immigrant seeking to improve her English to a student seeking knowledge to a tired worker in search of something to amuse and divert—the rainbow of library users will have an infinite number of hues. Somewhere in this future there is a library collection and a library service providing nutriment for the mind and soul of each and every human being.

Perhaps these statements seem Utopian—but they refer to a Utopia rooted in reality and in human needs. We know it is achievable because it is the projection of what exists. There are countless Americans for whom a library is central and whose lives have been changed, in ways great and small, by libraries and services provided by librarians and other library workers. What we must do is build on those achievements, create even better libraries, accept change as a positive force for our services and collections, and, in the words of the sage, be what we want to become—the guardian of our culture and an essential element of the empowering democracy of the mind.

Human Service

The American Library Association has issued a film that explores the issues brought to the forefront by the Americans with Disabilities Act (ADA).[1] It is, in part, a documentary dealing with real people (library users and library workers) with a range of disabilities. It also shows how libraries can offer those people a full range of services and employment opportunities. One moving scene shows the use of a public library by a mentally impaired man with an interest in and knowledge of birds. We see him using the section of books dealing with ornithology and picking out and reading his favorite titles. The depth of his feeling for the library and the accepting, unpatronizing way in which library staff help him are equally inspiring. Viewing this example of real library life, one cannot help but draw a contrast with the icy, isolated world of a virtual library.

It is very easy to see, in just this one instance of a multitude, the worth and variety of the relationships between libraries and individuals and libraries and society. Libraries are, and must remain, about human relationships in the service of individuals and communities. Libraries are, and must remain, complex, multidimensional webs of collections and services—each en-

---

1.   *People first: serving and employing people with disabilities*, Chicago: ALA Video, 1990.

hancing and complementing the others. It is only in recognizing and embracing that complexity and its attendant ambiguities that libraries will be able to continue their mission and thrive in an ever-changing society.

"And," Not "Or"

Print—books, magazines, newspapers—will survive as an important medium of communication for the indefinite future. Electronic publishing and dissemination will grow—probably at a great rate—and will displace print in the cases in which print is inferior, primarily compilations of data and short packages of information. The library will not be, and has never been, the primary source of information and data for most library users. Different libraries and library users will need different mixes of print and electronic communication. Thoughtful people will recognize and accept that the future is complicated and that there is no one answer to the communication of recorded knowledge and information. They will also recognize that most of the library's *information* services will be supported best by electronic technology and that its *knowledge* services will be supported best by physical collections supplemented by electronic resources. The efficient use of technology lies in applying it intelligently and appropriately to improve and enhance library services; to replace inefficient manual processes; and to deliver data and information when that delivery is more cost-effective than by "traditional" means. *The future means both print **and** electronic communication.*

Men and women will continue to write linear prose and treasure its qualities. Extended reading of linear texts will continue to be based on print-on-paper. Hypertext will increasingly be used where it serves best—not just in "help" systems but also to convey independent pieces of data and information and follow links between such pieces. *The future means both linear text **and** hypertext.*

Funding should improve for libraries, and particularly for strong support of the true expert systems in libraries—good librarians. Librarians must continue to pursue their two key missions, to serve their users and preserve the culture. At the same time, many users will get much of their information without the mediation of librarians—that has always been so. We should note that, almost invariably, direct use is predicated on the work of librarians in organizing, cataloguing, classifying, and providing guides to library resources.[2] *The future means both mediation by librarians **and** direct access.*

Most libraries, except for some in specialized areas, will *and must* continue to maintain and build strong collections of print and other media, in order to serve the essential needs of their users. Strong physical collections represent an incredible value in economic terms, as well as a critical resource for today and the future. Successful future libraries will build physical collections that, in combination with access to remote resources, meet the *real* needs of the users of the library and embrace all means of communication. Libraries will *and must* rely more heavily on access to materials (and nonmaterial information) that they do not own, and they must find ways to share the risks, costs, and benefits of such access. Librarians and those who fund libraries should not accept monolithic solutions to the problems of providing library materials and resources. In particular, they should reject the absurd notion that all library resources will be available in electronic form. *The future means both collections **and** access.*

It is essential that we understand the importance of the library *as place* while simultaneously using every means to reach beyond its walls. Librarians will do more and more of the latter both by providing some services electronically and giving access to much electronically recorded information. The library will, however, stand (in the future as in the past) as the heart of every good university, college, and school and the soul of every city and community. The future library needs to move beyond walls, not dispense with walls. *The future means a library that is both edifice **and** interface.*

---

2. Thomas Mann, *Library research models: a guide to classification, cataloging, and computers*, New York: Oxford University Press, 1993.

Speak Truth to Power

It is vital that libraries remain true to their own standards, missions, and goals. The surest path to irrelevance is to allow yourself to be defined by someone else. Librarians who accede to being called "information professionals" and libraries who go willingly into a subordinate role in a municipal "Leisure Department" or a university "Information Technology Division" have lost control of their destinies. This is not, as it is sometimes presented, an argument about names and, hence, a trivial matter. It goes right to the root of the identity of a profession and a centuries old cultural construct—the library—of great tradition, honor, and usefulness. A library by any other name does not smell as sweet, and a library that distorts its collections and services to bend to technological fads is no real library.

What should the guiding ideas be for a library that aspires to be successful? The librarian wishing to embrace the future should:

♦ remember that human service to human beings and communities is the prime reason for a library to exist;

♦ recognize that knowledge and understanding, not data and information, are the central concerns of libraries;

♦ defend the central ethical concerns of librarianship—equality of access to materials and resources; service; cooperation; and intellectual freedom;

♦ take pride in the way libraries and librarians have honored their mission for centuries and accept the weight of that mission.

It is easy to succumb to the propositions, driven by money and ideology, that the library is on the verge of irrelevance and that the only way to escape certain death is to change the fundamental nature of the institution. It is easy because librarians, seeing the marginalizing of school and public libraries in some areas and the crisis of the academic library, have felt the nagging doubt, the insidious self-questioning. Some librarians wonder if the futurists are right and if the "Information Age" will need libraries at all. Small wonder they do so since many university administrators, municipal authorities, and others who have power over the future of libraries have accepted many of the simplicities and falsehoods of the futurists.

To counter this phenomenon, librarians need two things— intellectual and professional self-confidence based on their own deeply-held feelings about the value of libraries, and the ability to obey the injunction to speak truth to power. It is our hope that this book has furnished some of the facts of library life and that it may help in marshaling the arguments all librarians will need in defending the central truths of libraries.

Rationality is the light with which libraries should approach their future. It is the lack of reason that has led to the superstitions of the library futurists. It is with the aid of reason that we will dispel their shadows. We should heed the words of the great painter:

> The sleep of reason produces monsters. Imagination deserted by reason creates impossible, useless thoughts. United with reason, imagination is the mother of all art and the source of all its beauty.[3]

Librarians can and should unite reason and imagination and, with their aid, create future libraries that will continue to serve and enrich individuals and the society in which they live.

Future libraries will be open to any and all suggestions about how to do things better and will be flexible enough to adopt new ways and new technologies when they are appropriate. It takes insight to distinguish between, on the one hand, the need to accept change in methods and, on the other hand, the need to preserve constancy of purpose and mission.

Librarians should never be afraid to defend the eternal mission of libraries—to collect, preserve, organize, and disseminate the records of the knowledge and information of humankind and to provide human services based on those records. Moreover, they should never be ashamed to defend and to show by example the core values—community, literacy, learning, service, reason, democracy, and intellectual freedom—upon which the culture of libraries is built.

---

3.   Goya, caption to *Caprichos*, #43, 179-?

Bibliography

All works cited within the text appear here, in addition to a few background articles and books.

Adler, Mortimer. *A guidebook to learning*. New York: Macmillan, 1986.

Advisory Panel for Scientific Publications. "The cost effectiveness of science journals." *Publishing Research Quarterly* 3 (Fall 1992): 72–91.

American library directory 1993–94. New Providence, N.J.: R. R. Bowker, 1994.

Bailey, Charles W., Jr. Electronic message on PACS-L, February 18, 1992.

Ballasch, Sandra. Electronic message on PACS-L, March 17, 1994.

Bar-Hillel, Yehoshua. *Language and information*. Reading, Mass.: Addison-Wesley, 1964.

Basch, Reva. "Books online." *Online*, July 1991, 13–23.

[Benchley, Robert.] "The coming of the movietone." *New Yorker*, July 14, 1928, 16–17.

Bent, Horace. *Bookseller*, July 30, 1993.

Billington, James H. "Electronic content and civilization's discontent." *Educom Review* 29 (September/October 1994): 22–25.

Bowker, R. R. "The work of the nineteenth-century librarian for the librarian of the twentieth." *Library Journal* 8 (September-October 1883): 247–250.

Buschmann, John. "Librarians, self-censorship, and information technologies." *College & Research Libraries*, May 1994, 221–228.

186   *Future Libraries*

California library statistics 1992/93. Sacramento: California State Library, 1993.

Cameron, Jamie. "The changing scene in journal publishing." *Publishers Weekly*, May 31, 1993, 23–24.

Caneva, Caterina. *Treasures of the Uffizi.* New York: Abbeville Press, 1994.

Carlyle, Thomas. *The hero as divinity,* Lecture I of his *Heroes, hero-worship & the heroic in history.* Berkeley: University of California Press, 1993.

Carroll, Lewis. *The complete works of Lewis Carroll.* New York: Modern Library, n.d.

Chadha, Sanjay R. "Virtual libraries continued." Electronic message on PACS-L, February 21, 1992.

Collier, Mel W., Anne Ramsden, and Zimin Wu. "The electronic library: virtually a reality." In *Opportunity 2000: 15th International Essen Symposium.* Essen: Universitatsbibliothek Essen, 1993, 135–146.

Crawford, Walt. *Current technologies in the library: an informal overview.* Boston: G. K. Hall, 1988.

Crawford, Walt. "Dreams, devices, niches, and edges: coping with the changing landscape of information technology." *Public-Access Computer Systems Review* 4, no. 5 (1993): 5–21.

Cringely, Robert X. *Accidental empires: how the boys of Silicon Valley make their millions, battle foreign competition, and still can't get a date.* Reading, Mass.: Addison-Wesley, 1992; New York: HarperBusiness, 1993.

Dickens, Charles. *Hard times.* New York: Knopf, 1992.

Directory of electronic journals, newsletters, and academic discussion lists. Washington, D.C.: Association of Research Libraries, 1994

Dougherty, Richard M., and Carol Hughes. *Preferred futures for libraries: a summary of six workshops with university provosts and library directors.* Mountain View, Calif.: Research Libraries Group, 1991.

Eco, Umberto. *The name of the rose.* San Diego: Harcourt Brace Jovanovich, 1985.

Eliot, T. S. *Burnt norton.* London: Faber, 1944.

Finks, Lee W. "Values without shame." *American Libraries,* April 1989, 352–356.

Florida library directory with statistics, 1993/94. Tallahassee: Department of State, Division of Library Services, 1993.

Franklin, Phyllis. "Scholars, librarians, and the future of primary records." *College & Research Libraries,* September 1993, 397–406.

Gorman, Michael. "The treason of the learned." *Library Journal* 119 (February 15, 1994): 130–131.

Hart, Michael. "Project Gutenberg: access to electronic texts." *Database,* December 1990, 6–9.

Hessel, Alfred. *Geschichte der Bibliotheken.* Translated, with supplementary material, by Reuben Peiss and published as *A history of libraries.* Washington, D.C.: Scarecrow Press, 1950.

Kent, Allen and others. *The use of library materials: the University of Pittsburgh study.* New York: Dekker, 1979.

Ketcham, Lee, and Kathleen Born. "Projecting serials costs: banking on the past to pay for the future." *Library Journal* 119 (April 15, 1994): 44–50.

Kirby, Steven. Electronic communication on PACS-L, March 3, 1992.

Koontz, Christie M. "Public library site evaluation and location: past and present market-based modelling tools for the future." *Library and Information Science Research* 14 (1992): 379–409.

Kountz, John. "Tomorrow's libraries: more than a modular telephone jack, less than a complete revolution—perspectives of a provocateur." *Library Hi Tech* 10, no. 4 (1992): 39–50.

"Kudzu, the write stuff." *Environmental Action* 25 (Winter 1994): 10.

Kurzweil, Raymond. "The virtual book revisited." *Library Journal* 118 (February 15, 1993): 145–146.

LC Information Bulletin, December 13, 1993, 466.

Lewis, Peter H. "Library of Congress offering to feed data superhighway." *New York Times,* September 12, 1994.

Lyall, Sarah. "Are these books, or what?: CD-ROM and the literary industry." *New York Times Book Review*, August 14, 1994.

Maddox, John. "Electronic journals have a future." *Nature* 356 (April 16, 1992): 559.

The magic of words: Rudolfo A. Anaya and his writings. Ed. Paul Vassallo. Albuquerque: University of New Mexio Press, 1982.

Mann, Thomas. *Library research models: a guide to classification, cataloging, and computers*. New York: Oxford University Press, 1993.

Max, D. T. "The end of the book?" *Atlantic Monthly*, September 1994, 61–71.

McCook, Kathleen de la Peña. "The first virtual reality." *American Libraries*, July/August 1993, 626–628.

McGarry, Kevin. *The changing context of information: an introductory analysis*. 2nd ed. London: Library Association Publishing, 1993.

Milton, John. *Areopagitica*. Santa Barbara: Bandanna Press, 1990. (First published in London in 1644.)

Mussman, Klaus. *Technological innovations in libraries, 1860–1960: an anecdotal history*. Westport, Conn.: Greenwood Press, 1993.

Nelson, Theodor. "Managing immense storage." *Byte* 13 (January 1988): 225–233.

Nirmala, N. "Master plan puts the byte on librarians: computer links will turn them into information brokers." *Straits Times Weekly Edition*, March 26, 1994.

Oxford English dictionary. 2nd ed. Oxford: Clarendon Press, 1989.

People first: serving and employing people with disabilities. Chicago: ALA Video, 1990.

Polly, Jean Armour, and Elaine Lyon. "Out of the archives and into the streets: American memory in American libraries." *Online* 16 (September 1992): 51–56.

Ranganathan, S. R. *Five laws of library science*. Madras: Madras Library Association; London: G. Blunt and Sons, 1931.

Roche, Marilyn M. *ARL/RLG interlibrary loan cost study: a joint effort by the Association of Research Libraries and the Research Libraries Group.* Washington, D.C.: The Association, 1993.

Santayana, George. *The life of reason.* 2nd ed., Vol. 1. New York: Scribner, 1927.

Schrage, Michael. "The next page in book publishing history should be a digitized one." *Los Angeles Times*, September 2, 1993.

Schwartz, Charles A. "Scholarly communication as a loosely coupled system: reassessing prospects for structural reform." *College & Research Libraries*, March 1994, 101–117.

Selth, Jeff, Nancy Koller, and Peter Briscoe. "The use of books within the library." *College & Research Libraries*, May 1992, 197–205.

Serials price projections 1995. Birmingham, Ala.: Ebsco Subscription Services, 1994.

St. Lifer, Evan. "Publishers of science journals win copyright fair use ruling." *Library Journal* 117 (September 1, 1992): 110.

Stein, Gertrude. *Reflection on the atomic bomb,* ed. Robert Bartlett Haas, vol. 1 of *Uncollected writings of Gertrude Stein,* Los Angeles: Black Sparrow Press, 1973.

Valauskas, Edward J. "Letter from the frontier." *Apple Library Users Group Newsletter*, April 1992, 42–44.

Valauskas, Edward J. "Paper-based or digital text: what's best?" *Computers in Libraries* 14 (January 1994): 45.

Vogl, Tom. Electronic message on PACS-L, February 20, 1992.

Wellisch, Hans. "Aere perennius?" In *Crossroads: proceedings of the first national conference of the Library and Information Technology Association.* Chicago: American Library Association, 1984.

"Where does the money go (and where does it come from)?" *CLR Reports*, new series (January 1994): 1–2.

White, Herbert S. "What do we want to be when we grow up?" *Library Journal* 119 (May 15, 1994): 50–51.

Whitman, Walt. *Complete poetry and selected prose and letters.* London: Nonesuch Press, 1938.

Wilson, David L. "Creating electronic texts." *Chronicle of Higher Education*, June 15, 1994.

Wurman, Richard Saul. *Information anxiety*. New York: Doubleday, 1989.

Index

About the Authors

Walt Crawford is a senior analyst at The Research Libraries Group, Inc., Mountain View, Calif., and has worked in library automation since 1968. A frequent writer and speaker on aspects of libraries, technology, and personal computing, Crawford has published 10 books and dozens of articles in those areas. He is past president (1992–1993) of the Library and Information Technology Association (LITA), a division of the American Library Association.

Michael Gorman, dean of library services at California State University, Fresno, is well known for his speeches and writings on bibliographic control, library automation, and library administration. He has taught graduate library science courses at the universities of Chicago, Illinois, and UC Berkeley. Gorman is the author or editor of a number of books and articles and the recipient of the American Library Association's Margaret Mann Citation and Melvil Dewey Medal.

This book is primarily set in Zapf Elliptical, a type family created for Bitstream, Inc., by Hermann Zapf. Zapf based the design, which is optimized for digital typography, on his own classic text face, Melior. Chapter and primary headings are set in Bitstream's Friz Quadrata BT. Special symbols are from Microsoft's Wingdings and ITC Zapf Dingbats. All type is True-Type.